AFFECTIVE DISORDERS

AFFECTIVE DISORDERS

PSYCHOANALYTIC CONTRIBUTION

TO THEIR STUDY

EDITED BY

PHYLLIS GREENACRE, M.D.

NEW YORK

International Universities Press, Inc.

CONTENTS

FOREWORD

The papers comprising this volume are part of panel discussions on affective disorders held at meetings of the American Psychoanalytic Association in 1950 and 1951. Those included in this small volume deal mainly with depression. There was no intention or attempt to cover the field of depression in a comprehensive or thoroughly organized way, but rather contributions were made by workers with special interest and experience, dealing with various aspects of the subject, sometimes from rather different points of view. Thus the spread or reach of the papers is such as to enrich, to stimulate, to illuminate and to suggest further avenues of study, to a rare degree, as well as to summarize much of the work of the past.

Depression, as a symptom, is as ubiquitous as life itself, and, in a mild degree, appears "naturally" as a reaction to loss which no life escapes. Its occurrence under these conditions is so regularly present as to be accepted as an accompaniment or sequel to loss which need hardly be questioned. It is, however, a positive, forceful affective state, though in a negative direction, as in contrast to apathy or indifference which it may superficially simulate, and it implies inherently some degree of identification of the subject with the object lost. It is certainly the intensity, the excessive duration and the domination of the organism by the affect, rather than its occurrence, which is pathological.

The peculiar enmeshment of the psychic state of depression and its manifestations in feelings of physical discomfort, or in actual impairment of physical functioning (slowness of motor activities and visceral functioning), or in specially emphasized physical equivalents bespeak either the extreme invasion of the affective state into *all* functioning with an ability to use and pull into its own service any channels of organismic strain and distress arising from other sources, or the real equivalents of the physical with the affective state, which should then give some further light on the source of the special intensity and force of depression when it appears as a sickness.

The foundation of depression in problems resulting from the failure of narcissistic supply (basically oral in nature) and the vicissitudes of the aggression aroused thereby has been described so repeatedly as to allow little doubt that this indeed must be an important and perhaps, in one form or another, the essential or nuclear disturbance. However this operates in the more complicated structure of the adult or older child, it may still be possible to get additional information from infancy itself.

[8]

The occurrence of depression as a psychic symptom, rather than merely as a physical condition, implies at least the early emergence of the ego. The work of Spitz and others, and especially the valuable clinical report of Bakwin on the fate of lonely babies, has indicated the all-importance for life itself of the maintenance of sufficient body relationship (primitive affective warmth) for the infant in the first months of life. Supremely valuable as these studies are, both in themselves, and in their focusing again on the primitive sources of disturbance—which we had for a time tended to disregard perhaps because of their seemingly overfanciful elaboration by some workers—there are, I believe, possible further behavioristic studies to be made on infants with follow-up studies in later life which might yield valuable insight into pathological affective states and rhythms. I have myself seen on a few rare occasions infants in the preverbal period who showed well-marked alternation of activity/mood cycles; and have seen also most spectacular pictures of this kind in extremely low-developed children: idiots in institutions. Unfortunately these latter observations of my own were made at a time when I was unequipped to study the subjects and could only be impressed by rather than really exploit the material. Are we to write these off, simply as constitutional, or can such states give us further understanding of the primitive source of more sophisticated disturbances? It has seemed to me since that there might be some "constitutional" or

early acquired patterned special relationship between motor activity and hunger—or total alimentary functioning—or even discrepancies in functioning between upper and lower gastrointestinal tract
in a fashion to make for alternating comfort and discomfort not merely on the model of hunger and
satiety (with or without rage), although undoubtedly influenced by this. I have further thought that
depressions of a deeper, more serious nature stand
shoulder to shoulder with schizophrenias and not far
removed from paranoid states. It has seemed to me
possible that the matrix of these severe disturbances,
including depressive psychoses of a cyclic nature, lay
in disturbances in that period at the very dawn of the
ego, roughly around six months and a little later,
when the primary process still reigns but aggression
of separation (and ego birth) becomes manifest. This
is the time of the special development of directed
extensor motion in the extremities, of dentition, and
of stronger visual focusing. There may then be a
realignment of these aggressive forces in relation to
the gastrointestinal demands and activities. It has
seemed that possibly different imbalances between
alimentary (I prefer this to the term "oral," as it
includes both oral and anal pressures) visual, and
peripheral motor functioning may occur. It would
seem that in the psychotic or severe affective states of
later life, the alimentary and the motor responses
bear an undue burden, whereas in the schizophrenic

conditions the visual—primitive intellectual—plays a much larger part.

It is indeed a heartening indication of the growth of analytic vision that it again concerns itself with psychoses and borderline states, although these conditions are not generally amenable to the formal psychoanalytic technique but require special flexibilities, modifications, and empathy.

PHYLLIS GREENACRE, M.D.

THE MECHANISM OF DEPRESSION[1]

EDWARD BIBRING, M.D.
Cambridge, Mass.

I

OUR SYSTEMATIC understanding of the dynamic structure of the depression began with Freud's first
attempt at the explanation of "Mourning and Melancholia" (1917), based on Abraham's earlier work
(1916). Freud points out that grief and melancholic
depression, though they have many clinical features
in common, differ in important aspects. In grief there
is an *actual* loss of an object, consequently a feeling
of the world being "poor and empty," but there is
no fall in self-esteem, no self-accusation. In melancholic depressions, there is usually an *emotional* loss
of object due to disappointment or related factors.
Consequently "the melancholic displays an extraor-
dinary fall of self-esteem, a loss of the ego: the ego

[1] Revised version of a paper read in May 1951 at the Annual Meeting
of the American Psychoanalytic Association as part of the panel on
Depressive and Manic States.

[13]

itself seems poor and empty, and is inclined to self-reproaches."

Freud offers various explanations for the difference. In the first place, simple depression, as represented by the uncomplicated grief reaction, is of an object-libidinal origin, in distinction from the narcissistic type of depression as exemplified by the melancholic form which may "extend beyond the clear case of a loss by death and include those situations of being wounded, hurt, neglected, out of favor, or disappointed, which can impart opposite feelings of love and hate." The disappointment by the (narcissistically chosen) object not only incurs a high degree of ambivalent feelings, but leads finally to a withdrawal of the libido from the object and to a reinforcing cathexis of the ego. This is achieved by the process of identification of the ego with the (emotionally) lost object. Freud accepted Abraham's proposition that the identification is carried out by the instinctual process of oral incorporation. This made it possible to trace the self-accusation back partly to feelings of guilt, to a need for self-punishment, partly and perhaps mainly to the aggressive feelings toward the object which had been turned against the patient's self as identified with the lost object.

Freud discusses among other problems that of the nature and origin of the *inhibition* so characteristic of the depressive states. According to him the inhibition is due to the "work of mourning" which absorbs nearly all libidinal energy, and which therefore accounts fully for the depressed person's loss of interest in the outside world. Freud extended this explanation also to the melancholic depression. The severe inhibition is explained by the fact that the "narcissistic wound" calls out for an unusually strong anticathexis which again results in the absorption of nearly all ego energy and consequently in an inhibition of functions including the interest in the external world.

Freud's explanations were further elaborated by various authors, particularly by Abraham and Rado. Abraham (1924) continued to explore his own and Freud's propositions within a detailed framework of the infantile libidinal development, particularly in regard to the oral and anal phases without reference to the ego aspect. He was the first to introduce the concept of a primal depression which develops in early childhood in reaction to a "severe injury of infantile narcissism through a combination of disappointments in love." The primal disappointment was assumed to have occurred in the later oral-cannibalistic stage of infantile development and was conceived of as oral frustration. The subsequent depressions follow the pattern established by the first.

Rado (1928) studied the influence of the varying phases and vicissitudes of the nursing situation on the infantile ego. Severe frustration on the oral level lowers the feeling of security and consequently the "self-esteem" of the infantile ego. Rado saw in the change from hunger (which he considered the deepest point of fixation in depression) to satisfaction the earliest model for a series of ego attitudes ranging from rage to depression, to self-punishment, to craving for affection, and finally to gratification and reconciliation, as observed in the manic and depressive states. Rado's contribution, though written in 1928, seems still to a large extent influenced by the concepts developed prior to the structural approach, which conceived of the ego as the "agent" of the instinctual drives, whose functions were predominantly modeled by and after the drives.

It would lead too far afield to quote the important contributions of other authors. In general, one can say that Freud's original distinction between simple (object-libidinal) and melancholic (narcissistic-ambivalent) depression was somewhat leveled down. On the one hand, the grief reaction frequently appeared complicated by ambivalence toward the lost object. On the other hand, increased observations suggested that identification occurred as a very frequent, if not regular, reaction to the (actual or emotional) loss of an object; that it was perhaps the only way of overcoming such a loss. Since identification (an ego function) was thought of as being closely linked up, if not identical, with oral incorporation (an instinctual process), it became a generally accepted proposition that the etiology of depression was intimately connected on the one hand with oral frustration, on the other hand with aggression in general, and oral aggression in particular.[2]

Fenichel's (1945) systematic survey of the literature on the subject can be considered as representative of the current conceptions of the various aspects of depression. He states that the simple as well as the melancholic forms of depression have in common a decrease in self-esteem. The clinical differences are viewed as stages in the course of the struggle to regain the lost self-esteem by various recovery mechanisms. A *slightly sad person* needs consolation, "narcissistic" (predominantly oral) "supplies" from the (external) objects. A *severe depression* represents the state into which "the orally dependent individual gets when the vital supplies are lacking." Such persistent lack usually leads to the familiar sequence of events: the libidinal withdrawal from the disappointing and therefore hated external object is followed by the "fateful" regression to the oral point of fixation and subsequent "incorporation" of the object. The struggle for the restoration of the self-esteem is now continued on the intrapsychic level, partly as "desperate attempts" to get from the introjected object (or the superego) the vital narcissistic supplies which originally were demanded from the real object partly by turning the object-directed aggression

[2] It should be stressed at this point already that the concept of identification is applied in the following paragraphs in terms of pure ego-function which may or may not have any connection with "oral incorporation."

toward oneself, particularly in the form of self-accusations and self-hatred.

Not all authors followed this line of thinking. Some maintained in principle Freud's original conception that the different clinical types of depression are based on essentially different mechanisms. Thus Edoardo Weiss (1944) separates clinically as well as theoretically a "simple" or "essential" type of depression from the "melancholic" type. According to him, simple depression is characterized by a decrease in the intensity of self-experience of the individual; "he is *less awake* and the external world conveys to him much less intense meaning than it does to other persons." Applying Federn's (1926) ego-psychological approach, Weiss states that the reason for the lowered ego feeling is to be found in the fact that "the libido is fixated to an object or goal which is rejected but cannot be relinquished," and that this continuous struggle finally exhausts the libido of the person to a degree which results in depression. Freud's explanation of the inhibition in depression by an absorption of ego energy is confined by Weiss to the "simple" depression.

In melancholic depression the patient's narcissism is "injured in the most obvious way." As a consequence, the main characteristics of melancholic depression are loss of self-esteem and the subsequent "development of self-hatred and self-accusations due to feelings of guilt and inferiority, irrespective of what the particular origin of such feelings might be."

[18]

The "ego feeling" in melancholic depression is, in contrast to the simple type, not lowered but increased. In brief, simple depression results from exhaustion of ego libido due to an unsolvable conflict (the "ego" is "empty") whereas melancholic depression is due to self-hatred as a consequence of an extensive loss of self-esteem through rejection.

Edith Jacobson (1946) discusses the impact of early disappointments in the parental omnipotence and of the subsequent devaluation of the parental images on the little child's ego formation. Such disappointment goes along with devaluation and "destruction" of the infantile self and causes a primary childhood depression which is repeated whenever in later years a similar disillusionment takes place.

However, Jacobson describes briefly another form of depression which she calls an "endogenous" or "a mild, blank" type and which she characterizes in terms similar to Edoardo Weiss, by a feebleness of the ego, "a feeling of disillusionment in life, a general physical fatigue and exhaustion, emotional emptiness, lack of initiative, and hypochondriac fears." In this type of depression, the feeling of guilt appears as a secondary formation, rather than as a primary or essential, etiological factor. Fenichel states also briefly that "many a simple neurotic depression" is due to "the circumstance that since the greater percentage of the available mental energy is used up in unconscious conflicts, not enough is left to provide the normal enjoyment of life and vitality."

[19]

This rather sketchy survey of the psychoanalytic literature on depression may suffice to demonstrate two major trends in explaining the structure and genesis of depression. According to one approach there exist at least two types of depression which differ clinically as well as theoretically; the first type (called simple, essential, endogenous, mild, blank, etc.) is represented on the one hand by the uncomplicated grief reaction (Freud), on the other hand by the depression primarily due to exhaustion of the "ego energy," for whatever reasons, and in whatever ways this may come about. The second (severe or melancholic) type is characterized by the familiar etiological syndrome: narcissistic injury, oral mechanisms of recovery, such as identification via incorporation and the concomitant turning of the aggression from the object against the self. According to the second approach, a loss of self-esteem is common to all types of depression. Consequently the clinical differences (ranging from simple sadness to the severe forms of melancholia) are explained by additional predominantly oral-aggressive etiological mechanisms which are employed in the course of the struggle for readjustment.

It is characteristic of the present state of affairs that Fenichel, notwithstanding the fact that he considers the existence of the exhaustion type of depression and occasionally hints at other possible types, nevertheless proceeds to define the general predisposition to depression in terms of an *"oral fixation which determines the later reaction to narcissistic shocks"* and "the narcissistic injury may create a depressive disposition because it *occurs early enough to be met by an orally oriented ego,"*[3] by what apparently is meant an "ego" which is tuned to external oral-narcissistic supplies. Fenichel takes also into consideration the reverse possibility, namely that shocks to the "self-esteem" in early childhood may secondarily create the decisive oral fixation in the sense that the *ego may become fixated to oral defense mechanisms,* but he did not pursue this possibility any further. Be it as it may, the same holds true of the phenomenon of elation which is also considered as a "narcissistic neurosis" like depression. "It too has its roots in oral eroticism. Incorporation and identification play a large role in both states" (Lewin, 1950).

In this article an attempt is made to approach the problem of depression from the ego-psychological point of view, which may be formulated in the thesis that depression is an ego-psychological phenomenon, a "state of the ego," an affective state. This refers to all "normal" and "neurotic" depressions, and probably also to what is called "psychotic" depression.

II

Before entering the discussion of the basic mechanism of depression, I should like to quote some

[3] My italics.

rather trivial instances of normal and neurotic depression, in order to elicit a primary model of depression.[4]

During the political crisis which preceded the recent war, many people felt depressed. Disregarding the specific ways in which the reaction was brought about in the various individuals, the common feeling was that the war, which they all did not want, seemed unavoidable, that it seemed impossible to do what they desired, namely to preserve peace.

Another example: a young girl fell into deep depression when general mobilization was ordered. She had the feeling that her old fear of merciless powers disrupting the peoples' lives had come true. The evidence of their existence undermined her former attempts to deny both the existence of the relentless powers and her fear of them. The fact that it was a power beyond her reach (the government, the world powers) made her feel completely helpless and depressed.

In the case of a man of about thirty, the persistent motive for the recurrent depression was not too easy to discover. He had a vivid feeling of his own existence whenever he had to cope with complicated, usually professional problems. When forced by the circumstances to do plain routine work for a longer

[4] It may be helpful to make it clear at this point that any descriptive classification of the various clinical pictures of depression is at first of no significance for the particular approach intended here since the question as to whether there is a common denominator in terms of the ego cuts across all clinical distinctions.

while, he regularly developed a depression. Analysis revealed among other factors that any routine performance made him feel insignificant, at a standstill, instead of proving his strength, or his growing stronger and more skillful by meeting the challenge of the complicated "test situation." His depression set in whenever he felt that his fear to remain weak and therefore unfit to meet "dangers" and "attackers," etc., seemed to come true.

One could quote many more trivial and complicated instances: the man who is depressed because he believes that he suffers from an inoperable cancer; the girl who finds herself alone on a weekend without a date; the patient who becomes depressed because he suffered an unexpected relapse into his neurosis, or because he felt that the warded-off "bad" impulses were still latently operative in him, or because he could not resist temptation; the man who develops a depression whenever he or his wife get sick or whenever he hears of people being tricked, people whom he considers as honest, but not a match for the "foxes," etc.

However trivial these instances may be, they seem to present a basic pattern which they have in common. In all these instances, the individuals either felt helplessly exposed to superior powers, fatal organic disease, or recurrent neurosis, or to the seemingly inescapable fate of being lonely, isolated, or unloved, or unavoidably confronted with the apparent evidence of being weak, inferior, or a failure. In all

[23]

instances, the depression accompanied a feeling of being doomed, irrespective of what the conscious or unconscious background of this feeling may have been: in all of them a blow was dealt to the person's self-esteem, on whatever grounds such self-esteem may have been founded. From this point of view, depression can be defined as the emotional expression (indication) of a state of helplessness and powerlessness[5] of the ego, irrespective of what may have caused the breakdown of the mechanisms which established his self-esteem.

The feelings of helplessness are not the only characteristic of depression. On further analysis of the quoted and other instances one invariably finds the condition that certain narcissistically significant, i.e., for the self-esteem pertinent, goals and objects are strongly maintained. Irrespective of their unconscious implications, one may roughly distinguish between three groups of such persisting aspirations of the person: (1) the wish to be worthy, to be loved, to be appreciated, not to be inferior or unworthy; (2) the wish to be strong, superior, great, secure, not to be weak and insecure; and (3) the wish to be good, to be loving, not to be aggressive, hateful and destructive. It is exactly from the tension between these highly charged narcissistic aspirations on the one hand, and the ego's acute awareness of its (real and

[5] The term "powerlessness" is not used in any objective or realistic sense, but entirely in its subjective meaning. Just as inferiority feelings do not prove any real inferiority of the patient, so the feeling of being powerless does not imply any real lack of power.

imaginary) helplessness and incapacity to live up to them on the other hand, that depression results.

In the first group the depression sets in whenever the fear of being inferior or defective seems to come true, whenever and in whatever way the person comes to feel that all effort was in vain, that he is definitely doomed to be a "failure." In the second group of persisting tensions (schematically described as the desire to be strong), and the depression is due to the shocklike (actual or imaginary or symbolic) evidence that this goal will never be achieved due to the ego's weakness, that one is doomed to be a "victim" (with regard to dangers, or merciless powers and their unconscious implications). In the third group of tensions (the desire to be loving, not to be aggresive, etc.), the narcissistic shock (blow to the self-esteem) is due to the unexpected awareness of the existence of latent aggressive tendencies within the self, with all the consequences involved, and this in spite of the fact that one had tried hard to be loving and not to hate, not to be "evil."

These three sets of conditions are, of course, not exclusive of each other but may, under certain circumstances, coexist in varying combinations in the same individual and at the same time. Though the persisting aspirations are of a threefold nature, the *basic mechanism of the resulting depression appears to be essentially the same.* According to this view, depression is primarily not determined by a conflict between the ego on the one hand and the id, or the superego, or the environment on the other hand, but stems primarily from a tension within the ego itself, from an inner-systemic "conflict." Thus depression can be defined as the emotional correlate of a partial or complete collapse of the self-esteem of the ego, since it feels unable to live up to its aspirations (ego ideal, superego) while they are strongly maintained.

A suitable illustration of the intimate connection between the state of helplessness and depression is offered by the girl quoted above who reacted with depression to general mobilization. Her infantile (but "denied") fear that there are inaccessible merciless powers disrupting the peoples' lives seemed to be substantiated by the political events. The government and the international powers were so far beyond her reach that she felt utterly helpless and depressed. However, her reaction to various individuals who—in her opinion—threatened to disrupt her life was characteristically different: she did not develop any depression but a violent rage which sometimes led to physical attack. It is also characteristic that she felt relieved immediately after having succeeded in hurting (mostly verbally) the disappointing love object. This served as proof that she had at least as much power over the object as she was afraid the object might have over her, in brief, that she was not helpless, that she could "get even" with them. This feeling of power over the object made any rage as well as any depression unnecessary. She became depressed, however, when she found herself confronted

[26]

with forces beyond her reach, that is, when the ego in all its relative power was made to feel helpless and consequently any attempt to cope with the situation meaningless.

One could ask at this point whether the simple, i.e., uncomplicated grief reaction fits in the proposed scheme. In the instance of an actual loss of love object, the resulting tension can be described as a longing for the lost object and love, and a wish to retrieve the loss (maintenance of object and goal). The depression, sometimes accompanied by a feeling of pain, appears to derive from the fact that here too the ego is confronted with an inescapable situation, since it does not have the power to undo the loss. Observation shows, e.g., that an exacerbation of the grief reaction occurs whenever certain conditions bring the loss and the inability to retrieve it acutely into awareness.

III

According to the conception exposed here, basic depression represents a state of the ego whose main characteristics are a decrease of self-esteem, a more or less intense state of helplessness, a more or less intensive and extensive inhibition of functions, and a more or less intensely felt particular emotion; in other words, depression represents an affective state, which indicates a state of the ego in terms of helplessness and inhibition of functions.

[27]

To clarify this further, I should like to compare depression with similar affective states, such as depersonalization and boredom. They seem to be phenomenologically related and it is sometimes difficult for the patients to keep them apart.

The main complaint of depersonalized persons refers to not having any feelings, to being blocked emotionally, being "frozen" which is often accompanied by feelings of unreality of the self, of behaving like automatons, etc. Clinical observations show that depersonalization often develops in place of an acute outburst of anger, and for that reason it has been classified as "defense mechanism," though it is difficult to define the actual process. One may describe it more generally as acute blocking in *statu nascendi* of overwhelming tensions (aggression and others) *within* the ego, which goes along with certain changes in the feeling function of the ego which are experienced as various forms of inhibition. A related type of "depersonalization" is represented by the well-known behavior in situations of danger. The persons involved describe a state of cold alertness and clarity of mind and a feeling of acting like an automaton, yet mostly in highly rational manner. When the danger has passed, many of these individuals show a delayed reaction in form of tremors, crying spells, sweating, palpitation, and other expressions or equivalents of anxiety. The anxiety which threatened to overwhelm the ego was blocked in *statu nascendi* or "bound" (anticathected) as long as the danger

[28]

lasted, and liberated only when the danger subsided. In both instances of depersonalization, the ego protects itself actively against the danger of being overwhelmed by strong tensions by blocking their further development, as a measure of defense. In both instances a modification of the feeling function of the ego takes place which can be described under the category of inhibition.

The dynamic conditions of boredom, which too represent a state of particular mental inhibition, have been discussed by Fenichel (1934) and others, most recently by Greenson (1953). According to the definition of Lipps (quoted by Fenichel) boredom is a painful feeling originating in a tension between a need for mental activity and the lack of adequate stimulation, or the ego's incapacity of being stimulated to such activity. Fenichel adds the hypothesis that this inability is the result of repression of the instinctual "aims." The need for activity is felt, but since the "aims are repressed," there is an incapacity to develop direction from within. This forces the person to seek a solution from external stimulation. He is, however, not capable of adequate stimulation from outside, because the gratifications offered are either too much removed from the (unconscious) aims to serve as substitutes, or because they come so close to the warded-off aims that they incur inhibition. A certain similarity with depression and a characteristic difference becomes obvious. The (unconscious) goals are maintained in depression as well as in boredom, but the ability to reach them is interfered with in boredom by the repression of the true goals and the rejection of substitutes because they are either inadequate or prohibited. The result is a lack of directions, the inability to bring about goal-directed behavior in spite of many attempts in this direction, and subsequently a feeling of emptiness and boredom. In depression the ego is shocked into passivity not because there is a conflict regarding the goals, but because of its own incapacity to live up to the undisputed narcissistic aspirations.

The conditions leading to boredom as well as to depression could be observed in case of a female patient who passionately liked to travel and who was highly excited when she started to make arrangements for a journey to a "new" place. She was not interested in traveling to "civilized" countries, but preferred those which seemed "exotic" and therefore exciting to her, such as the oriental countries. She used to prepare for such travels, reading copious literature about them and particularly about the customs of the people. But she repeatedly went through the same experience: she was all enthusiastic at the beginning; after a while, however, she began to lose interest, felt bored and finally depressed. Analysis revealed that she had particular conceptions of the "noncivilized" peoples, that the customs and habits in which she was (unconsciously) interested were of sexual nature. Her conscious-unconscious hopes to find amorous adventures were predominantly concerned with perverted practices which she was eager to learn—mainly for narcissistic reasons. Since her repressed wishes could not be gratified by the various substitutes, her initial excitement subsided very soon and she felt disappointed and bored. The fact that she went through this same experience with a certain regularity made her feel increasingly depressed, i.e., helpless with regard to the fulfillment of her narcissistic expectations.

The same patient reacted with depression whenever she was told that a person had died in early years. It was one of her painful fears that she would die before her life finished its natural course, which meant before certain aspirations had been fulfilled. She felt that people should only die when they had lived their lives to a meaningful end. One unconscious meaning of this fear was that she could pass away before having learned to know what she wanted so badly, the sexual secrets of the "children of nature." Here too, the depression was due to a feeling of helplessness inevitably induced by the evidence that people did die young in age before their lives were "fulfilled," before they "knew all," before they could catch up with the grownups. Cases of involutionary melancholia often expose a similar psychology. The curtain falls before certain expectations are fulfilled, before the "happy end" is enacted.

Many patients whose main symptom consists in chronic boredom show a similar pattern. They get occasionally excited out of proportion about new impressions or new activities which seem to hold a promise in regard to unconscious narcissistic aspiration, but they lose interest very soon and fall back onto the chronic feelings of boredom, when the expected promising and "shattering" great event did not materialize. The feeling of boredom is finally followed by depression when a sense of helplessness and inescapability is added. These individuals show the same sequence of reactions in analysis, particularly at the beginning, since they transfer very soon the narcissistic fantasy of a great, all-pervasive, all-liberating experience onto the treatment situation. Disappointment, boredom, depression follow in quick succession to be repeated at similar constellations in the course of treatment.

To summarize: depersonalization, boredom, and depression represent affective states and states of mental inhibition. In *depersonalization,* usually aggressive tensions are acutely barred from emotional and motor expression by a—little understood—general blocking of the feeling functions as a measure of defense. In *boredom* libidinal strivings are maintained but actively prevented from (substitute) gratification. The inhibition of functions in boredom refers to the blocking of the development of goal-directed (or need-directed) behavior. In boredom as well as in depersonalization the self-esteem of the person remains outside of the sphere of conflict. In *depression* the narcissistically important aims are perpetuated, but the narcissistic core of the ego, its self-esteem, is broken down, since the ego functions —which usually serve the gratification of the particular narcissistic strivings—appear to be highly inadequate, partly due to reality factors, partly due to internal reasons. *why?* *such as?*

Freud (1926) defines inhibition as a "restriction of functions of the ego" and mentions two major causes for such restrictions: either they have been imposed upon the person as a measure of precaution, e.g., to prevent the development of anxiety or feelings of guilt, or brought about as a result of exhaustion of energy of the ego engaged in intense defensive activities. He quotes as illustration of a general though transitory inhibition of ego function an obsessional patient, who "used to be overcome by a paralyzing fatigue which lasted for one or more days whenever something occurred which should obviously have thrown him into a rage." Freud adds: "We have here a point of departure from which we may hope to reach an understanding of the condition of general inhibition which characterizes states of depression, including the gravest form of them, melancholia."

The inhibition in depression as elaborated in this paper does not fall under either category; it is neither explained as due to a measure of precaution nor to a depletion of energy. It is rather due to the fact that certain strivings of the person become meaningless— since the ego appears incapable ever to gratify them.

This is further supported by a comparison of the

[33]

state of depression with the state of fatigue. Is it apparently not by chance that depressions are so often subjectively experienced as fatigue, so much so that fatigue is considered to be an "equivalent" of depression. It is probably also not by chance that physical exhaustion through stress and strain, or disease, is frequently accompanied by feelings of depression. The depressed person, severely disappointed in himself has lost his incentives and gives up, not the goals, but pursuing them, since this proves to be useless; he is "tired." The physically exhausted person is incapable of any effort; he is depressed. At least, one can formulate that in both cases vitality, the vigor in pursuing goals, is considerably lowered or nearly completed inhibited.

To clarify the status of depression still further, it may be helpful at this point to compare depression with the feeling of anxiety, particularly since the latter has been brought in close connection with the feeling of helplessness (Freud). Both are frequent—probably equally frequent—ego reactions, scaling from the mildest, practically insignificant forms to the most intensive, pathological structures. Since they cannot be reduced any further, it may be justified to call them basic ego reactions. From the point of view elaborated here, anxiety and depression represent diametrically opposed basic ego responses. Anxiety as a reaction to (external or internal) danger indicates the ego's desire to survive. The ego, challenged by the danger, mobilizes the signal of anxiety and prepares for fight or flight. In depression, the opposite takes place, the ego is paralyzed because it finds itself incapable to meet the "danger." In extreme situations the wish to live is replaced by the wish to die. (This does not mean, however, that anxiety and depression are exclusive of each other. A person may be anxious in one respect and depressed for other reasons, since the collapse of self-esteem is in many cases only a partial one. Or depression may follow anxiety, the mobilization of energy may be replaced by a decrease of self-reliance, etc.)[6]

It is hardly possible to discuss depression without taking into account the phenomenon of elation, which also extends from the mildest form to those of a very intense, pathological degree. Though elation frequently occurs as a compensatory reaction to states of anxiety as well as to states of depression, it nevertheless has to be considered as a basic (independent) state of mind in the ego's inventory of responses to internal or external stimuli. In contrast to depression, elation is the expression of an actual or imaginary fulfillment of the person's narcissistic aspirations.

Summarizing one can say that there are four basic ego states: (1) the state of balanced narcissism (nor-

---

[6] Be it as it may, the very fact of depression, of the wish to die, or of "the ego letting itself die" (Freud) represents a problem to any biologically oriented psychology. Perhaps one could at this point venture the hypothesis that in cases of physical—and emotional—exhaustion, the feeling of fatigue as well as of depression serve as warning signals not to exert oneself any longer.

[35]

mal self-esteem), the secure and self-assured ego; (2) the state of excited or exhilarated self-esteem, the triumphant or elated ego; (3) the state of threatened narcissism, the anxious ego; and (4) the state of broken-down self-regard, the "inhibited" or paralyzed, the depressed ego. In other words, depression is on the same plane as anxiety and other reactive ego states. It is—essentially—"a human way of reacting to frustration and misery" whenever the ego finds itself in a state of (real or imaginary) helplessness against "overwhelming odds."

IV

It follows from the definition of depression that it is not warranted to define the predisposition to depression as exclusively consisting "in oral fixations which determine the later reaction to narcissistic shocks," or to generalize that the depressive predisposition is created by a narcissistic injury "met by an orally oriented ego." The "orally dependent type" which constantly needs "narcissistic supplies" from outside, represents perhaps the most frequent type of predisposition to depression, which is not surprising if one takes into consideration the fact that the infant has actually no power over its objects and the necessary supplies it has to receive from them, that it is entirely dependent on the benevolence of the environment for the gratification of his needs and maintenance of his life. Frequent frustrations of the infant's oral needs may mobilize at first anxiety and anger. If frustration is continued, however, in disregard of the "signals" produced by the infant, the anger will be replaced by feelings of exhaustion, of helplessness and depression. This early self-experience of the infantile ego's helplessness, of its lack of power to provide the vital supplies, is probably the most frequent factor predisposing to depression. I should like to stress the point that the emphasis is not on the oral frustration and subsequent oral fixation, but on the infant's or little child's shocklike experience of and fixation to the feeling of helplessness.

The narcissistic aspirations developed on the oral level, or subsequently built on it, may be generally defined as the need to get affection, to be loved, to be taken care of, to get the "supplies," or by the opposite defensive need: to be independent, self-supporting. Depression follows the painful discovery of not being loved or not being independent, whenever this discovery regressively evokes the primary feeling of helplessness with regard to the gratification of these narcissistic needs.

A strikingly different picture is offered by the anal-sadistic phase. In contrast to the child on the oral level, the child of the anal phase has often to defend certain of his strivings and cherished sources of gratification against the interference by the objects. The oral child is completely dependent on the objects, it is therefore easily made to feel helpless. The child of the anal phase usually has acquired a certain independent ego strength, a certain capacity to control his body and his instinctual interests as well as the objects. It has learned not only how to exert sphincter control but is also capable of saying "no," of defying grownups, of mobilizing various forms of aggression as a defense against the interfering objects. The narcissistic aspirations characteristic of this phase refer to mastery over the body as well as over the drives and the objects. When in reaction to the sometimes intense aggression, feelings of remorse and guilt are developed, together with a fear of punishment, the corresponding aspirations will consist of the wish to be good, not to be resentful, hostile, defiant, but to be loving, not to be dirty, but to be clean, etc. Depression, i.e., the feeling of relative powerlessness or helplessness, will refer to the lack of control over the libidinal as well as aggressive impulses or over the objects, to the feelings of weakness ("I am too weak ever to control the forbidden impulses or the interfering objects"), or to the feelings of guilt ("I shall never succeed in being good and loving, I am destined to be hateful, hostile and defiant, and therefore evil").

The phallic phase shows again a different type of ego involvement. Competitive strivings within the oedipal situation are intimately linked up with exhibitionistic and sadistic needs to defeat the rival and to be admired by maternal images or substitutes. In the phallic stage, therefore, the narcissistic aspirations stem mainly from the competitive situation, the wish to be admired, to be center of attention, to be strong and victorious, not to be defeated, and so forth. Depression may result, e.g., when the fear of being defeated and ridiculed for one's shortcomings and defects, or the fear of retaliation, etc., seem to come true and the ego proves too weak to prevent the inevitable.

To summarize: what has been described as the basic mechanism of depression, the ego's shocking awarenes of its helplessness in regard to its aspirations, is assumed to represent the core of normal, neurotic and probably also psychotic depression. It is further assumed on the basis of clinical material that such traumatic experiences usually occur in early childhood and establish a fixation of the ego to the state of helplessness. This state is later on regressively reactivated whenever situations arise which resemble the primary shock condition, i.e., when for external or internal reasons those particular functions which serve the fulfillment of the important aspiration, prove to be inadequate.

It has been mentioned above that as far as observations suggest the child of the oral phase is more frequently exposed to the traumatic impression of helplessness, particularly since it is actually helpless. Similar reactions may be established by any severe frustration of the little child's vital needs in and beyond the oral phase, e.g., of the child's needs for affection (Abraham), or by a failure in the child-mother relationship of mutuality (Erikson, 1950) or by an early disappointment in the parental omnipotence (Jacobson, 1946), etc.

It is finally assumed that all other factors which determine the different clinical pictures of depression represent accelerating conditions or "complications" superimposed on the basic mechanism by the oral defense mechanisms and their sequelae. More precisely, one has to make a clearer distinction between: (1) the basic or essential mechanism of depression (fall in self-esteem due to the awareness of one's own real or imaginary, partial or total insufficiency or helplessness; (2) conditions which predispose to and help to bring about depression; (3) the attempts at restitution associated with depression; (4) conditions which complicate the basic type of depression such as aggression and orality; and (5) the secondary use which may be made—consciously or unconsciously—of an established depression (e.g., to get attention and affection or other narcissistic gratification).

To discuss these points briefly: (1) According to the viewpoint adopted here, *depression represents a basic reaction* to situations of narcissistic frustration which to prevent appears to be beyond the power of the ego, just as *anxiety represents a basic reaction* of the ego to situations of danger. Depression is defined as being primarily an ego phenomenon, i.e., as being essentially independent of the vicissitudes of aggression as well as of oral drives. Since depressions

frequently appear to be linked up with self-reproaches, the concept of depression became synony-
mous with self-accusation and self-destruction to such
a degree that nearly every depression was viewed as
resulting from the turning of originally object-directed aggression against self. The same holds true of
the relation between depression and oral striving.
Here, too, the frequent observation of oral implications in depression led to the definition of the predisposition for depression in terms of oral fixation.
It is true that an "orally oriented person," who is
dependent on external "supplies" for the maintenance of his self-esteem, is prone to narcissistic in-
juries and oral recovery mechanisms, but to reverse
this statement is not justified.

It should be stressed that the conception of depression presented here does not invalidate the
accepted theories of the role which orality and aggression play in the various types of depression. It
implies, however, that the oral and aggressive strivings are not as universal in depression as is generally
assumed and that consequently the theories built on
them do not offer sufficient explanation, but require
a certain modification: it is our contention, based on
clinical observation, that it is the ego's awareness of
its helplessness which in certain cases forces it to turn
the aggression from the object against the self, thus
aggravating and complicating the structure of depression.

If the conception presented here is correct, then

any condition which forces a feeling of helplessness upon the infantile ego may create a predisposition to depression. The conception of the exhaustion type of depression comes very close to the viewpoint presented here with the difference that the emphasis is not on the exhaustion of libidinal energy but on the state of helplessness of the ego confronted with an insolvable situation.

(2) In general, one may say that everything that lowers or paralyzes the ego's self-esteem without changing the narcissistically important aims represents a condition of depression. External or internal, actual or symbolic factors may consciously or unconsciously refute the denial of weakness or defeat or danger, may dispel systems of self-deception, may destroy hope, may reveal lack of affection or respect or prove the existence in oneself of undesirable impulses or thoughts or attitudes, or offer evidence that dormant or neutralized fears are actually "justified," and so forth; the subsequent results will be the same: the individual will regressively react with the feeling of powerlessness and helplessness with regard to his loneliness, isolation, weakness, inferiority, evilness or guilt. Whatever the external or internal objects or representations of the narcissistically important strivings may be, the mechanism of depression will be the same. The narcissistic shock may be mild or severe, focal or extensive, partial or complete, depending on whatever peripheral or central narcissistic aspirations are

involved. These factors will contribute to the extent and intensity of the depression as well as the possibilities, the means, or the tempo of recovery.

Our scheme seems not only suitable to bring a certain order into the variety of configurations resulting in depression, but also permits a clearer conception of the therapeutic effort. From a theoretical as well as therapeutic point of view one has to pay attention not only to the dynamic and genetic basis of the persisting narcissistic aspirations, the frustrations of which the ego cannot tolerate, but also the dynamic and genetic conditions which forced the infantile ego to become fixated to feelings of helplessness. Its major importance in the therapy of depression is obvious.[7]

(3) The same conditions which bring about depression, in reverse serve frequently the restitution from depression. Generally one can say that depression subsides either (a) when the narcissistically important goals and objects appear to be again within reach (which is frequently followed by a temporary elation), or (b) when they become sufficiently modified or reduced to become realizable; or (c) when they are altogether relinquished; or (d) when the ego recovers from the narcissistic shock by regaining its self-esteem with the help of various recovery mechanisms (with or without any change of object and goal).

[7] This is to some degree in agreement with Karen Horney (1945) who stressed the necessity of analyzing not only the "conflicts," but also the "hopelessness."

Finally (e) defense can be directed also against the affect of depression as such. This usually results in apathy or hypomania. Certain observations suggest that apathy is due to a "blocking" of the depressive emotion, to the mechanism of depersonalization in a (usually chronically) depressed person; whereas certain types of hypomania represent a reaction formation to depression, usually combined with a denial of the causes of depression (Helene Deutsch, 1927, 1933).

(4) The most frequent complication of the basic structure of depression can be found in the large group of orally dependent people who thrive on "oral-narcissistic supplies" and collapse when these are lacking, or who in reaction to severe frustration regress to the oral mechanism of restitution, the most fateful recovery mechanism consisting in the "incorporation" of the objects in cases of severely ambivalent attitudes toward it.

The correlation between depression and aggression on the one hand, mania and aggression on the other, can be observed in the fantasies as well as in the occasional acting out of depressive patients. On recovery from depression by regaining self-esteem and the feeling of strength, aggressive impulses are released and directed against the object world. Under such conditions, e.g., a female patient frequently had the fantasy of walking along the street, with a large sword in her hand and cutting off the heads of the people passing by to the right and left. The sequence of depression, self-accusation, hypomania, aggression against the outside world, could be clearly observed in the patient. But as much as her aggressive fantasies were secondary to her exaggerated self-esteem, so was the turning of aggression against the self—particularly in form of self-hatred—secondary to the lowering of self-esteem. On the basis of similar observations it seems justified to generalize that the turning of aggressive impulses against the self is secondary to a breakdown of the self-esteem. It is ultimately due to the feeling of powerlessness and helplessness (often combined with masochistic tendencies) that the ego "surrenders" to the superego and accepts punishment. We observe at least in certain instances the opposite tendencies of the ego, namely, to defy and "repress" the demands of the superego as long as the ego feels strong and powerful in its rebellion. There are cases where no feeling of guilt and no self-accusation developed (though one would normally expect it) because the "bad" deed was to a high degree narcissistically gratifying, whereas guilt and self-reproaches develop when the gratification subsides. However, there are depressions which are not accompanied by any self-aggression and there are cases of angry self-hatred which do not show any manifest signs of depression and which are not the result of a defensive action but demonstrate rather a hostile nonidentification with or "rejection" of a given weakness of the self. Such persons hate or resent certain features in themselves in the same way as they hate or resent the same traits in another person. Finally, there is a decisive difference between the "ego killing itself" and the "ego letting itself die." Only in the first case aggression is involved. Giving up the struggle because one is tired and feels helpless is not identical with self-destruction.

(5)It is hardly necessary to discuss the conscious and unconscious secondary gains which many patients derive from a depression. This may proceed on the external as well as internal level. By demonstrating their sufferings they try to obtain the "narcissistic supplies" which they need, or they may exploit the depression for the justification of the various aggressive impulses toward external objects, thus closing the vicious circle.

BIBLIOGRAPHY

Abraham, Karl: (1916) The first pregenital stage of the libido. In *Selected Papers on Psycho-Analysis.* London: Hogarth Press, 1927.
—— (1924) A short study of the development of the libido. In *Selected Papers on Psycho-Analysis.* London: Hogarth Press, 1927.
Bergler, Edmund: (1945) On the disease entity boredom ("alyosis") and its psychopathology. *Psychiatric Quarterly, 19.*
Brierley, Marjorie: (1937) Affects in theory and practice. *International Journal of Psycho-Analysis, 18.*
Deutsch, Helene: (1927) Ueber Zufriedenheit, Glück und Ekstase. *Internationale Zeitschrift für Psychoanalyse, 13.*
—— (1933) Zur Psychologie der manisch-depressiven Zustände, insbesondere der chronischen Hypomanie. *Internationale Zeitschrift für Psychoanalyse, 19.*
Erikson, Erik H.: (1950) *Childhood and Society.* New York: W. W. Norton & Co.
Federn, Paul: (1926) Some variations in ego feeling. *International Journal of Psycho-Analysis, 7.*
Fenichel, Otto: (1934) Zur Psychologie der Langeweile. *Imago, 20.*
—— (1945) *The Psychoanalytic Theory of Neurosis.* New York: W. W. Norton & Co.

Ferenczi, Sandor: (1919) Sunday neuroses. In *Further Contributions to the Theory and Technique of Psycho-Analysis*. London: Hogarth Press, 1926.

Freud, Sigmund: (1914) On narcissism: an introduction. In: *Collected Papers, IV*. London: Hogarth Press, 1925.

—— (1917) Mourning and melancholia. In: *Collected Papers, IV*.

—— (1918) *Introductory Lectures to Psychoanalysis*. New York: Boni and Liveright, 1920.

—— (1923) *The Ego and the Id*. London: Hogarth Press, 1927.

—— (1926) *The Problem of Anxiety*. New York: W. W. Norton & Co., 1936.

Friedlander, Kate: (1940) On the longing to die. *International Journal of Psycho-Analysis, 21*.

Garma, Angel: (1947) Psychoanalytic investigations in melancholias and other types of depressions. In *The Yearbook of Psychoanalysis, III*. New York: International Universities Press.

Gero, George: (1936) The construction of depression. *International Journal of Psycho-Analysis, 17*.

—— (1939) Zum Problem der oralen Fixierung. *Internationale Zeitschrift für Psychoanalyse, 24*.

Glover, Edward: (1939) Second analysis of affects. *International Journal of Psycho-Analysis, 20*.

—— (1949) *Psychoanalysis,* 2nd edition. New York: The Staples Press.

Greenson, Ralph R.: (1949) The psychology of apathy. *Psychoanalytic Quarterly, 18*.

—— (1953) On boredom. *Journal of the American Psychoanalytic Association, 1*.

Horney, Karen: (1937) *The Neurotic Personality of Our Time*. New York: W. W. Norton & Company, Inc.

—— (1945) *Our Inner Conflicts*. New York: W. W. Norton & Company, Inc.

Jacobson, Edith: (1943) The oedipus conflict in the development of depressive mechanisms. *The Psychoanalytic Quarterly, 12*.

—— (1946) The effect of disappointment on ego and superego formation in normal and depressive development. *Psychoanalytic Review, 33*.

Klein, Melanie: (1935) Contribution to the psycho-genesis of the manic-depressive states. In: *Contributions to Psycho-Analysis 1921-1945*. London: Hogarth Press, 1948.

Kris, Ernst: (1950) On preconscious mental processes. *Psychoanalytic Quarterly, 19*. Also in *Psychoanalytic Explorations in Art*. New York: International Universities Press, 1952.

Landauer, Karl: Equivalente der Trauer. *Internationale Zeitschrift für Psychoanalyse, 21*.

Lewin, Bertram D.: (1950) *The Psychoanalysis of Elation*. New York: W. W. Norton & Co.

Lorand, Sandor: (1937) Dynamics and therapy of depressive states. *Psychoanalytic Review, 20.* Also in *Clinical Studies in Psychoanalysis.* New York: International Universities Press, 1950.

—— (1946) Neurotic depression. Chapter 8 in *Technique of Psychoanalytic Therapy.* New York: International Universities Press.

Nunberg, Herman: (1924) Ueber Depersonalisationszustände im Lichte der Libidotheorie. *Internationale Zeitschrift für Psychoanalyse, 10.*

Pfister, Oskar: (1930) Schockdenken und Schockphantasieren in hoechster Todesgefahr. *Internationale Zeitschrift für Psychoanalyse, 16.*

Rado, Sandor: (1928) The problem of melancholia. *International Journal of Psycho-Analysis, 9.*

—— (1953) The psychoanalysis of pharmacothymia (drug addiction). *Psychoanalytic Quarterly, 22.*

Rapaport, David: (1942) *Emotions and Memory.* New York: International Universities Press, 1950.

Spitz, René A.: (1937) Wiederholung, Rhythmus, Langeweile. *Imago, 23.*

—— (1946) Anaclitic depression. In *The Psychoanalytic Study of the Child, II.* New York: International Universities Press.

Weiss, Edoardo: (1944) Clinical aspects of depression. *Psychoanalytic Quarterly, 13.*

Winterstein, Alfred von: (1930) Angst vor dem Neuen, Neugier und Langeweile. *Psychoanalytische Bewegung, 2.*

Wulff, M.: (1932) Ueber einen interessanten oralen Symptomenkomplex und seine Beziehung zur Sucht. *Internationale Zeitschrift für Psychoanalyse, 18.*

Zilboorg, Gregory: (1935) Zum Selbstmordproblem. *Internationale Zeitschrift für Psychoanalyse, 21.*

—— (1937) Considerations on suicide with particular reference to that of the young. *American Journal of Orthopsychiatry, 7.*

—— (1946) Manic-Depressive Psychoses. In *Psychoanalysis Today,* edited by Sandor Lorand. New York: International Universities Press.

CONTRIBUTION TO THE METAPSYCHOL OGY OF CYCLOTHYMIC DEPRESSION

Edith Jacobson, M.D.
New York, N. Y.

I

THIS PAPER is offered as a contribution to the meta-psychology of cyclothymic depression and will extend lines of thinking pursued in a few previous studies.[1]

I choose as my point of departure our panel discussion on mania, of the 1950 Midwinter Meeting.[2] On this occasion, Nunberg confessed his amazement at the trends of the discussion. As I understood him, he considered the manic-depressive conditions he had seen to be psychotic states, inaccessible to psychoanalytic investigation, and requiring hospitalization rather than psychoanalytic treatment. In fact, Nunberg reminded us emphatically that mania and mel-

[1] See Jacobson (1943, 1946, 1947).
[2] For an abstract of the Panel on Mania and Hypomania, see *Bulletin of the American Psychoanalytic Association*, 7:265-276, 1951.

ancholia are not neurotic but psychotic disorders, after all. In principle, I appreciated this reminder, but I should like to express my disagreement with Nunberg at a decisive point.

Great clinical psychiatrists, such as Kraepelin and Bleuler, have not failed to point to the great number of cases of "simple depression" that do not manifest psychotic symptoms in the sense of delusional ideas or hallucinations, but nevertheless belong to the manic-depressive group.[3] Since these cases are easily mistaken for neurasthenic or psychoneurotic, somatic or psychosomatic disturbances, they are frequently referred to the analyst. Usually such a patient is amenable to psychoanalytic approach, even when in a depressed or hypomanic state, provided, however, that we know we are dealing with a basically psychotic case and do not neglect differential-diagnostic considerations. From the therapeutic point of view a correct diagnosis will guide our choice of methods of treatment. Scientifically, we have even better reasons for adhering to a clear distinction between neurosis and psychosis. In a previous paper (1947) I have discussed this issue at some length. The assumption

[3] M. Katan, who reserves the term "psychotic" for conditions that show definite signs of a break with reality, would probably characterize such patients as remaining in a prepsychotic stage. In view of the fact that they mostly manifest the typical triad of symptoms—periods of depressed mood, of inhibition of thinking, and of psychomotor retardation, or the opposite, respectively—I have found it useful, and furthermore in accordance with clinical psychiatry, to emphasize the psychotic nature of their pathology. The term prepsychotic will be applied to the characterological predisposition to this disease.

that psychosis, in contradistinction to psychoneurosis, represents not only a mental but an unknown psychosomatic process is well founded. This hypothesis, first of all, will act as an incentive to a sound collaboration of physiological, biological, and psychological research on the problem of psychosis. And, regarding the psychological aspects, which are our subject matter, I believe, indeed, that we can make an inroad into the psychology of psychoses only by studying the specific predisposition to these disorders and the specific structure of the psychotic conflict, defenses, and restitution mechanisms.

To be sure, in cases of depression a clear differential diagnosis may often be difficult or impossible. But valuable diagnostic criteria may be gained by focusing on the psychosomatic, "endogenous" features in the questionable syndrome. I refer not only to the symptoms that impressed even Freud as having somatic rather than psychological origin: the insomnia, the anorexia, the amenorrhea, the loss of weight, the metabolic disturbances, or the frequent gastrointestinal or cardiovascular psychosomatic symptoms. What I wish to emphasize especially are the psychosomatic features in the depressive retardation. True cyclothymics will experience their slowing up quite differently from the way depressive neurotics experience their inhibitions. Cyclothymics seem to be aware that there is a somatic quality to this phenomenon. They commonly feel that the retardation, as well as the keyed-up state, befalls them

[51]

like a physical illness. They experience it as strange
to their nature; as something the sound part of their
personality may watch with some detachment and
even control to a certain point. Frequently they are
unaware of their depressed affective state and com-
plain only about their mental and physical fatigue
and exhaustion. They may compare the slowing up
to a fog settling down in their brain; to a veil drawn
over their thinking; to unsurmountable walls blocking their feelings, their thinking, and their actions,
etc., etc. This subjective inner awareness of an endogenous process is often more pronounced in simple
depression than in manic-depressive cases with bla-
tant psychotic symptoms, because in the former the
ego is not so fully immersed in the pathological
process.

When we combine clinical observation of these
endogenous phenomena with a comparative psychoanalytic study of various neurotic and psychotic types
of depression, we will certainly come to the conclusion that it is correct to regard the mild and the
acute psychotic types as a nosological unit, which
should be distinguished from the great variety of
neurotic depressive states.[4]

---

[4] For reasons of precision it may be emphasized that Edward Bibring
in his paper on depression (*This Volume*, pp. 13-48) obviously applies
the term "mild or simple depression" to neurotic types of depression,
whereas this term in my paper refers to "simple" in contrast to "acute"
psychotic depression only.

II

The central psychological problem in depression appears to be the narcissistic breakdown of the depressed person: his loss of self-esteem, or, to put it more broadly, his feelings of impoverishment, helplessness, weakness, and inferiority; or, in the melancholic type, of moral worthlessness and even sinfulness. I believe that a better understanding of this problem can arise only from a further metapsychological clarification of the development of secondary narcissism. This I will try to do in the first part of this paper. Since the discussion must be restricted to the issues that are most pertinent to the following investigation of depression, it will focus mainly on the concept of self-representations and on their infantile development in relation to that of the superego and the object-representations. Unfortunately, I cannot avoid a repetition of familiar facts.

The development of secondary narcissism represents a complex and much broader process than is suggested by defining it rather imprecisely as a cathexis of the ego with narcissistic libido. Actually, this development involves the beginning formation of the system ego proceeding with the gradual discovery and distinction of the self and the objects and with the constitution and cathexis of self- and of personal object- and thing-representations. This process is normally promoted by affectionate paren-

[53]

tal love as much as by frustrations, prohibitions, and demands. By supporting the neutralization of sexual and aggressive drives, these influences contribute to the maturation of our feelings, thinking, and acting and lead eventually to the establishment of aim-inhibited object-relations and of sublimations through identifications with the love-objects in the ego and superego. Thus the new systems—the ego and, later on, the superego—are gradually vested with libidinous, aggressive, and neutralized psychic energy, which is used for a lasting cathexis of object- and self-representations.

I introduced above the term "self-representations," which I was gratified to see also mentioned by Hartmann (1950). It is a concept that I have long found indispensable for the study of psychosis, and in particular of depression and the depressive disturbance of self-esteem. When, years ago, Richard Sterba (1947) suggested the term "ego-representations," which was not accepted at that time, he evidently had the same concept in mind. Unfortunately he had been unaware as yet of the differences between the ego and the self. Only recently Hartmann (1950) pointed to the necessity to distinguish more clearly than Freud himself had done between the self and the system ego. In fact, from what was said above we conclude that secondary narcissism should not be defined as a cathexis of the ego with narcissistic libido. The ambiguous use of the terms cathexis, narcissism, and narcissistic libido, as in this definition, can easly become a source of confusion. The system ego is not only cathected with narcissistic libido. It is endowed with psychic forces that are used for the cathexis of object- and self-representations and for the corresponding ego functions. Hence, narcissistic libido is only that part of the libidinous energy in the system ego that is used for the cathexis of the self-representations, in contradistinction to the object-representations. Gratifications, gained from sexual or other ego activities, are object-libidinous, in so far as their goal is the satisfaction on personal and thing objects; they are narcissistic gratifications, in so far as they aim as well at the raising of the libidinous cathexis of the self-representations and at the satisfaction of the self. And, finally, what we call "narcissistic identification," the mechanism that plays such an important role in melancholic depression, must be defined not as an identification of the ego with the object but as partial or total fusions of self- and object-representations in the system ego. In this type of identification the ego does not assume the characteristics of the love-object. The self is experienced or treated as though it were the love-object. As regards the superego, it would be correct to say that the ego-ideal part of it is normally cathected with libido, while the critical superego cannot be described as cathected but as equipped with libidinous and aggressive drives, which are exclusively used for the cathexis of the self-representations and, in case of severe depression, e.g., may be discharged on the real self. This example also suggests the necessity for more precise distinctions between real objects and self and their respective mental representations and between ego attitudes or actions in the outside world and changes in the cathexes of object- and self-representations. Again, it is Richard Sterba (1947) who pointed out years ago that the cathectic processes need not necessarily correspond with the behavior in the realistic object world. We shall see further on that these distinctions are of particular importance for the understanding of the depressive defense mechanisms.

We shall now consider the development of the self-representations. The concept of our self issues from two sources: first, from a direct awareness of our inner experiences and, second, from indirect self-perception, that is from the perception of our bodily and our mental self as an object. Since the self-representations are only partly the product of our self-cognizant functions, they will never be strictly "conceptual" but remain under the influence of our subjective emotional experiences even more than the object-representations.

The nuclei of the early infantile self-images are our first body-images and sensations. Like the primitive object-images, our concept of the self is at first not a firm unit. It is fused and confused with the object-images and is composed of a constantly changing series of self-images, which reflect mainly the incessant fluctuations of our mental state. With advancing psychosexual and ego development and the maturation of reality testing, a more stable, uniform, and realistic concept of the self and a lasting, firm cathexis of the self-representations will normally be established. By a realistic concept of the self we mean a concept that mirrors only or mainly the state and the characteristics of our ego: of our conscious and preconscious feelings and thoughts, wishes and impulses, attitudes and actions. It will be unrealistic if the self-representations assume the coloring of infantile self-images, which have remained cathected in the unconscious.

Normally, the early infantile images of the self and of the love-objects develop in two directions. On the one hand, they grow into consolidated realistic object- and self-representations, whose site is in the system ego. On the other hand, they also form the core of the superego and ego ideal.

The still insufficient distinction between object and self at the beginning of superego formation explains why the deep unconscious kernel of the superego represents fusions of images of both, the love-objects and the self. Since the infantile object- and self-images are the carriers of the child's first value measures, the latter become integrated in the superego and survive, in its deep layers, even normally, to a high extent. The development of the infantile value system is reflected in the leading fears of the infantile developmental stages. The fear, first, of loss of pleasure, then of loss of the love-object; later on, of castration, and finally of the superego, i.e., of a loss of moral value, corresponds to the infantile value concepts first of pleasure versus unpleasure, then of a powerful (protective, supportive) versus a weak love-object, later of phallic strength versus phallic weakness, and, eventually, of moral power versus moral inferiority.

The most decisive step in this development is the stage when the child becomes aware of his biological helplessness and dependency situation. The loss of belief in his own omnipotence will teach him to prefer security to pleasure and, hence, to accept a strong love-object that gives him security, though it may deprive him of pleasure. This experience prepares the child for his oedipal conflict, during which the wish for phallic strength will defeat his desire for genital pleasure.

This step is of particular importance in the development of masochism and depression. We know that the helpless little child with a hostile, rejecting mother will rather accept and submit to this powerful though aggressive love-object than give it up altogether.

The distinctions between truth and falseness, correctness and incorrectness, reason and unreason will accomplish a maturation of the concepts of value and will lead, partly at least, to the victory of the reality principle over the pleasure principle and to the acceptance of what is realistic and reasonable. This development promotes the building up of realistic object- and self-representations and of judgment functions in the ego, of the ability correctly to evaluate the outside and inside reality.

Self-perception is an ego function. Self-judgment, though founded on the subjective inner experience and on objective perception by the ego of the physical and mental self, is partly or even predominantly exercised by the superego, but is also partly a critical ego function whose development weakens the power of the superego over the ego. Self-esteem is the emotional expression of self-evaluation and of the corresponding libidinous or aggressive cathexis of the self-representations.

The foregoing discussion leads to the conclusion that self-esteem does not necessarily reflect the tension between superego and ego. Broadly defined, self-esteem expresses the discrepancy between or accordance of the wishful concept of the self and the self-representations. Disturbances of self-esteem may arise from any sources and represent a very complex pathology: on the one hand, a pathology of the ego ideal and of the self-critical ego and superego functions; on the other hand, a pathology of the ego functions and of the self-representations. Increase or inhibition of libidinous or aggressive discharges, a libidinous impoverishment or enrichment of the self from outside or inside, from somatic, psychosomatic, or psychological sources may reduce or increase the libidinous or aggressive cathexis of the self-representations and lead to fluctuations of self-esteem and corresponding affective vacillations, that is, to depressed or elated states.[5]

We will end the discussion of secondary narcissism with some remarks about the relations between ego functions or ego inhibitions, and the cathexis of the self- and object-representations. Since action aims at a gratification of the real self on an external object (thing or person), normal functioning of the ego presupposes a sufficient and evenly distributed libidinous cathexis of both the object- and the self-representations. The action will be stimulated by an initial overcathexis of the latter, which will encourage and guarantee the success of the action. The ensuing increase of object-cathexis puts the drive into motion, determines its direction, and leads to its completion. An insufficient libidinous object-cathexis and/or an initial insufficient libidinous self-cathexis may result in partial inhibitions. A libidinous over-cathexis of the self along with an aggressive over-cathexis of the object will lead to narcissistic and sadistic attitudes to the object; the opposite will correspond with masochistic behavior. But a major withdrawal and shift of cathexis from the object- to the self-representations will lead inevitably to passivity or to general inhibition of the ego functions. The

[5] I may emphasize the differences between Bibring's opinions and the ones expressed here. Bibring also points to the multitude of sources from which depressed states may arise. However, whereas he refuses to ascribe the central part in the pathology of depression to aggression and its vicissitudes, I am convinced, on clinical and theoretical grounds, that this view is correct.

[60]

best example of a normal process of this sort is the state of happy passivity after sexual object-gratification or the sleeping state. In these two cases the libidinous cathexis has been withdrawn from the object- to the self-representations, or the self, respectively. The most pathological counterparts are depressive retardation and depressive stupor. The difference between these last states and the first lies in the fact that, because of the libidinous impoverishment and the rise of destructive energy, in this last case, aggressive, instead of libidinous, cathexis has been withdrawn from the object and turned to the self.

III

The brief discussion of secondary narcissism, and in particular of the self-representations and their genetic relations to the object-representations and to superego formation, has been intended to prepare us for the metapsychological study of cyclothymic depression. But before approaching the main topic, I have first to sketch shortly my general metapsychological conception of psychosis.

In contradistinction to neurotics, psychotics evidently seek a solution to their psychosexual conflicts in a regressive escape, which involves not only instinctual regression but a severe regressive process in the whole personality organization. As a patient after recovery from a schizophrenic episode put it dras-

tically: "I ran and ran and ran, back to the womb."
Because of their inherited constitution and their
infantile history of emotional deprivations and instinctual overstimulation and/or frustration, these
patients are evidently predisposed to such a total
regressive process by an arrested, defective ego and
superego development. It seems to me that the central element in this predisposition is a neutralization
of libidinous and aggressive forces, insufficient for
normal maturation, for a lasting cathexis of object-
and self-representations, and the maintenance of firm
ego and superego identifications. In the prepsychotic
personality the self- and object-representations and
the ego ideal will not be sharply separated; they
will retain attributes of early infantile object- and
self-images, and they will be carriers of primitive infantile values, such as those described in the first
part of this paper. The superego will not be a firmly
integrated system. It will be personified, unstable in
its functions, and will tend either to assume excessive
control of the ego or to disintegrate, dissolve, and
merge with object- and self-representations. It will
be easily reprojected on the outside world. The superego, the object- and self-representations will be
prone to a regressive fragmentation, to a splitting up
again into primitive early images and, on the other
hand, to fusions with one another. There will be a
tendency to react to conflicts with the object world
not by ego defenses against unacceptable strivings
but by withdrawals and shifts of libidinous and ag-

gressive cathexis, not only from one object to the other and from personal object- to thing-representations, but from the object- to the self-representations and the reverse. The onset of the psychosis proper is characterized by a dangerous, irresistible defusion or, as I would prefer to say, deneutralization, of instincts, which unleashes a furious struggle for supremacy between the libidinous and the destructive forces.[6] Whatever sets it going, this struggle may lead eventually to a fatal libidinous impoverishment, an accumulation of sheer aggression, and a dispersion of the defused instincts in the whole self. I suspect that the "endogenous" psychosomatic phenomena in psychosis, to which I pointed above, arise with the development of such a state.

Psychologically, the psychotic process is probably set in motion by a reactivation of infantile conflicts centered primarily around both parental love-objects or their substitutes, but spreading to the whole object world, conflicts, which the defective ego of the prepsychotic is unable to master with the help of neurotic defenses. It resorts to attempts at a conflict solution by shifts, first of the libidinous, then of the aggressive cathexis from the object- to the self-representations by renewed efforts to recathect the objects and finally by increasing fusions of both.

[6] We may well speculate that the underlying psychosomatic processes in psychoses result in a reduction and exhaustion, or else in an insufficient reproduction, of libidinous drives, which enforces a reversal of the neutralization process and changes the absolute proportion between libido and aggression in favor of the latter.

This goes along with a severe regressive distortion of the object- and self-representations, leading to their breakdown and their eventual dissolution into primitive images, in the system ego. The ego and superego identifications will disintegrate and be replaced by "narcissistic identifications," i.e., by regressive fusions of superego, of self- and object-images. These processes may reach the point of a collapse of the psychic systems. They find expression in schizophrenics' experiences not only of "the end of the world" but also of a loss of identity or feelings of having died.

Naturally, severe disturbances of the sense of reality, i.e., of the perception of and the judgment regarding the object world and their own self, will develop. The ego functions and the emotional relationships with the real objects will deteriorate; there will be misinterpretations and inadequate responses to the object world, etc., etc.

The psychotic defense mechanisms will aim at the maintenance and/or restitution of object- and self-representations. First, the real object world will be used for this purpose. The psychotic will attempt to save himself by support from without: by a strengthening of his perceptive and motor functions, by looking for emotional and ideational stimulants from the outside world. If this effort fails, he will retreat from the object world. Regressively revived, primitive object- and self-images, which have found their way to consciousness, will merge and join with remnants of realistic concepts to form new units. In this way, delusional object- and self-representations will be built up, in disregard of reality, and will be reprojected on the outside world.

Psychoanalytic literature on psychosis still lacks studies of both groups of psychoses, schizophrenia and cyclothymia, from a common and comparative point of view.

Possibly it is the depth of regression that determines the development of a manic-depressive or a schizophrenic psychosis. Manic-depressives seem to have reached a higher level in the differentiation and integration of the psychic systems, to begin with. Consequently, the acute regressive process during their episodes does not go so far as in schizophrenics. Usually, it does not lead to a complete disintegration of the personality, but is reversible. It stops at a point that still allows a rather complete recovery. Bleuler has described as a characteristic difference between the schizophrenic and the manic-depressive that the fears of the first refer to disasters occurring at the present time, those of the latter to future catastrophes. I believe that this difference is an expression of the metapsychological distinction that in the schizophrenic the object- and self-representations, in the system ego, break down actually to the point of dissolution, whereas the manic-depressive only feels threatened. His anxieties may be severe, but they are not true states of panic. His delusions in manic or melancholic states show characteristic differences from schizophrenic delusions, which, I believe, prove this point. As to the suicide of the melancholic, we may remember, Freud (1915) said that the love-object is shown to be more powerful than the self. I may venture to add that in the suicidal act the self, too, regains a feeling of power and achieves a final, though fatal, victory.

IV

We shall now turn to the special study of the phenomena that I have highlighted, as they appear in the manic-depressive personality. When we have an opportunity to observe cyclothymic patients before their break or during free intervals, we are often impressed by the richness of their sublimations. We are also surprised to see that as long as they are not sick, they may be delightful companions or marital partners, a feature that Bleuler mentioned especially. In their sexual life they may show a full genital response, and emotionally, in contradistinction to schizoid persons, a touching warmth and unusual, affectionate clinging to people they like. No doubt, these persons have developed to the level of emotional object-relations and are potentially able to function extraordinarily well. But though they do not manifest a lack of inner resources, they seem to suffer from a specific ego weakness, which shows in their remarkable vulnerability, their intolerance toward frustration, hurt, and disappointment.

Freud (1917) underlined the contradictory fact that these persons show simultaneously the tendency to too strong fixations to their love-object and to a quick withdrawal of object cathexis. He pointed to Otto Rank's remark that the object choice of these persons must have been, to begin with, on a narcissistic basis, which permits them to regress easily to the narcissistic identification with the love-object described in "Mourning and Melancholia." This is true indeed. Manic-depressive persons manifest a particular kind of infantile narcissistic dependency on their love-object. What they require is a constant supply of love and moral support from a highly valued love-object, which need not be a person but may be represented by a powerful symbol, a religious, political, or scientific cause, or an organization of which they feel a part. As long as their "belief" in this object lasts, they will be able to work with enthusiasm and high efficiency. Actually, however, these patients tend to make a masochistic choice of their partners or "causes" and to establish a life situation that sets the stage for their illness in that it is bound to disappoint them. Gero (1936) pointed out that manic-depressives belong to the masochistic personality type. When we have an opportunity to observe both, the patient and his partner, we frequently find that they live in a peculiar symbiotic love relationship to each other; they feed on each other. Not so rarely we find partners who are both manic-depressive and who break down alternately.

[67]

Or else, the partner of the manic-depressive may be an oral type of a different variety.

As a point of departure for the metapsychological study of this personality structure and of the development of the depressive conflict and defense and restitution mechanisms, I have chosen a short dream of patient B., a physician who was at the beginning of a depression. It had been precipitated by the alarming news that his mother had a cancer of the uterus, which required immediate operation. During the last years B. had developed depressive states with a paranoid tinge, with feelings of tiredness and exhaustion, and with a series of psychosomatic and hypochondriacal symptoms and fears. They had begun at the time he detected that his wife had to undergo a gynecological operation which might affect her fertility.

B. dreamed that he had lost two of his "excellent" teeth. As they fell out, a fine thin silver cord that held them together went to pieces. B.'s immediate interpretation was that the two teeth represented himself and his mother and that the connecting structure was the umbilical cord by which he was still attached to her. If his mother should die, he would feel as though he had lost his own self. The silver cord also represented his weak personality, which, in the case of her death, would break down.

When this patient was not depressed, he would manifest a rather conspicuous self-inflation. He would express his feelings of being very good-looking, bright and smart, as "excellent" in his field as his teeth were. In these states he would also talk incessantly of his worship for his mother, of her unending kindness and generosity, her great intelligence, her physical and mental strength. He had married his wife because she seemed to resemble his mother. Neither woman in any way corresponded to this ideal picture. They were neurotic, overanxious, clinging women, and, as mentioned above, both suffered from a chronic gynecological condition. The patient had managed for years to deny their weaknesses, including their physical handicaps. He himself had gone through several serious illnesses to which he had regularly responded with a depressive state along with hypochondriacal complaints and fears. At other times, the patient would exhibit an uncommon pride in his body.

His dream of the loss of his teeth referred to an experience in his adolescence when the patient had lost a tooth because his mother had neglected the adequate dental care of her children, in the same way as she had neglected her own present illness until it was almost too late for help. At the time of his tooth trouble, the boy had to take the matter into his own hands. He had found a dentist who extracted the tooth, supposedly because it could not be saved. I may interject here that B. went into medicine because the mother's only brother as well as his own older brother, a father substitute, were physicians. Both men he had greatly admired. Hence, medicine, his vocation, represented an ideal derived from both parental love-objects. His mother had told him repeatedly how she had nursed and cured him during his early childhood diseases. But an outstanding early childhood trauma had been the death of his maternal grandmother whom neither uncle nor mother had been able to cure. And both, uncle and brother, had been very gifted and promising young men who failed completely in their careers.

During the dream session the patient began to express his deep resentment of his mother's and his wife's inability to take proper care of their own health and that of their children. He would blame his mother for his severe childhood diseases, which had probably been neglected as much as his teeth. As the session proceeded, the patient started derogating the whole medical profession for its utter impotence. He talked of prominent but incompetent doctors who drew a fortune from their patients' ignorance. And, finally, he indulged in severe self-reproaches: he blamed himself for being an incompetent, neglectful physician, uninterested in his patients and unable to cure them. He ended the session with an expression of deep guilt feelings toward his mother, whose sickness he had ignored and neglected and diagnosed too late to save her. He left in a very depressed state.

The dream and dream material and the corresponding emotional reactions during this one session show in a nutshell the prerequisites for and the development of the depressive conflict.

The superficial symbolic interpretation by the patient informs us already about the pathogenic core of the manic-depressive personality. The thin, fragile silver cord in the dream indicates the weakness of his ego, resting on the intimate bond between himself and his mother. The two teeth are the symbol of his love-object- and his self-representations. The one tooth, representing his mother, is his own. The two teeth are connected. In other words, we see what I regard as characteristic of these patients: the insufficient separation between the love-object- and self-representations, the lack of distinct boundaries between them, which accounts for the patient's too strong fixation to the parental love-objects. The self-representations extend, so to speak, to the object-representations; both show insufficient maturation and stability. The patient gauges his love-objects and himself by infantile value measures, predominantly by their omnipotent physical power and invulnerability. These standards are embedded in his high-flung ideal of a competent, in fact omnipotent, physician, who devotes his whole life to the rescue of his patients. In the patient's associations, we observe also the personification of his ego ideal, its insufficient distinction from the ideal parental image. He talks indiscriminately of the value or worthlessness of the whole medical science and profession and of the individual physicians who represent parental images.

His example shows, furthermore, how in manic-depressives all ambitions and pursuits revolve only about representations of the overvalued parental love-objects, which extend, as it were, to the whole world. This is why all their ego functions fail when the love-object is depreciated. Frequently we observe that manic-depressives live on their ideals or their idealized partners rather than on their own real self. They exhibit an unusual pride in their idealizations as though their own idealism would per se turn them into valuable human beings. We may add that the "idealism" of the manic-depressive differs greatly, in type, from that of the schizophrenic. The latter is abstract, removed from personal objects, the former is concrete and, as in the above-described case, mostly attached to a personal representative object. This accounts for the seeming "realism" of the manic-depressive, which clinical psychiatrists, such as Lange, have described.

We shall now investigate how the depressed state developed in our patient. This time it was precipitated by his mother's sickness, but at other times it had developed when he himself became sick or met with failure in his work, with financial difficulties, or with disappointments in his love life. In other words, his depressive states would be precipitated by a failing of his love-object or of himself. But the analysis showed that, in either case, the patient felt hurt and blamed the love-object for it. In fact this patient expressed with unusual clarity his feeling that all his achievements or failures were due to the effectiveness or failure of his "intuition"—in German, *Einge-bung;* that is, all achievements or failures were the result of what had been given to him. He regarded his ego functions not as his own productions but as reproductions of what he had received. We understand that in disregard of his potential abilities, his self-representations retained the infantile conception of a helpless self, drawing its strength from a powerful, ideal love-object. He tried to keep the image of this love-object hypercathected, by constantly depriving the self-image of its libidinous cathexis and pouring it on the object-image. He then had to bolster his self again by a reflux of libido from the love-object image. These continuous cathectic fluctuations found expression in corresponding emotional vacillations. In his actual attitudes he would show a mixture of conceited and humble, sadomasochistic and protective behavior to the love-object and simultaneously demand continuous evidence of the latter's value, power and devotion. This is the basis of the "symbiotic" type of relationship to which I pointed above.

This position is inevitably unstable and facilitates easy, rapid, and drastic cathectic changes on the slightest provocation. Against this danger the manic-depressive has to protect himself by strong pathological safeguards, essentially by the denial mechanisms so beautifully described by Lewin (1950). He can maintain a lasting libidinous overcathexis of the love-object image only by constant efforts at denial of his own intrinsic value and of the weaknesses of the real love-object, i.e., by a continuous, illusory overestimation of the love-object and an equally illusory under- or overestimation of himself. If he meets with disappointment or failure, the denial mechanisms will either break down or have to be so fortified that the patient may go into a manic state, which—in contradistinction to schizophrenic feelings of grandeur—represents, I believe, a state of lasting participation of the self in the imagined omnipotence of the love-object. The manic can afford to discharge his aggression fully and diffusely. Since, by his denial of the existence of unpleasure and destruction, the whole world will become a valley of unending and indestructible pleasure, his aggression can do no damage.[7]

In case the denial mechanisms fail, the patient's first reaction will be to master the narcissistic injury and build up his self by disparaging the love-object in a way as illusory as he had previously glorified it. He will try to repair the hurt by switching the whole aggressive cathexis to the object image and the libidinous cathexis to the self-image. In adolescence this mechanism was still effectual in our patient. He

[7] A patient in a hypomanic state, which terminated a nine-month period of depression, told me that she felt so voracious: she would like to eat up everything—food, books, pictures, persons, the whole world. When I jokingly and with deliberate provocation remarked that this seemed to be quite bad and dangerous, what would she do if everything were eaten up, she said, highly amused: "Oh no, the world is so rich, there is no end to it. Things are never finished. I cannot hurt anybody, or anything."

[74]

asserted himself by derogating his neglectful mother and by reactive identification with her ideal image. Thus he went ahead and took care of his tooth, instead of and in spite of his mother. But he indicated in his dream that unconsciously he regarded his success—for good reasons—as a failure: he actually lost his tooth, which in the dream was equated with his own self and his mother. In fact, manic-depressives may react to success in love or work in the same way as to failure: with either a hypomanic or manic state or with a depression. Their reaction depends on what the success will mean: an aggressive self-assertion by derogation and destruction of the love-object, or a present from the powerful love-object. Their inability to accept success is not always or not only an expression of their moral masochism and of their guilt conflict. One of my depressive patients regularly responds to achievements by a struggle between feelings of tremendous pride and of rising anxiety and emptiness. He feels as though the most precious thing in life were gone; life will be empty forever. He loses his interest in his previous endeavors and may end by feeling that his whole work has been worthless anyhow. This response is only more intense and pathological than the well-known attitude of narcissistic people who value an object as long as they cannot get it and depreciate it as soon as they have got it. But the manic-depressive cannot bear a self-assertion through derogation of his love-object. He tries to avoid such a situation by keeping the valued love-object at a distance, as it were, which protects it from deflation. The simultaneous libidinous hypercathexis of the object clearly distinguishes this attitude from the schizoid remoteness. Since the love-object has to stay unattainable, he may avoid success by delaying a final achievement or the real consummation of a love relationship, for which he has deseperately struggled.

Evidently, he is so afraid of a lasting self-inflation at the expense of the love-object, because it might lead to a complete libidinous withdrawal and a letting loose of all his severe hostility on this one object. His fear of a "loss of the object" is fear of a destructive absorption of the "good, powerful" object-image by the self-image. Here is a situation that induces an immediate and intense need to retrieve his old position. He will be overperceptive of any flaw in his achievements and use it to confirm his own weakness and to reinstate the strength and value of the object. This is why success afflicts the manic-depressive in the same way as failure. Either may arouse an initial hostile derogation of the love-object, which cannot be tolerated and which yields to a rapid reversal, undoing, and denial of the previous situation.

There will be an immediate, increased reflux of aggression from the love-object to the self-image; but by this time the pathological process may have proceeded so far that the patient will be too depleted of libido to sufficiently recathect the object. All he can achieve may be an aggressive devaluation of both:

of himself and of his love-object. He will return to his position of participation, but in the worthlessness instead of the value of the love-object. Many patients, especially those with chronic simple depression, and many depressive children, may present this picture. They manifest a general pessimism, disillusionment, and lack of interest in life and in themselves. Everything has become worthless, unpleasurable, or empty. They maintain a continuous denial of the world's and their own value.

I postulated in a previous paper (1947) that I regard this as the primary depressive disturbance, which may be distinguished from the secondary attempts at defense and restitution. Some patients give evidence indeed of very intense efforts to recathect and build up the love-object image again and to regain their original unstable equilibrium.

We will now investigate the defenses that the patient uses for this purpose. Since his libidinous resources are fading, his first line of defense will be to turn to the real object world for support. He will try to resolve his inner conflict by help from without. He wants to use the love of an outside person to whom he has attached his ideal object-image as a stimulant for his failing ability to love. This is the stage when the patient, in his frantic endeavor to stop the depressive process, will develop a persistent and increasing clinging to the person he has chosen for this purpose. He will gather all his available libido and pour it on this one person in a desperate

[77]

appeal to give such convincing evidence of unending love and indestructible power and value as to evoke a libidinous response in himself and, in this way, enable him to re-establish an ideal object-image that cannot be deflated and destroyed. It is a phase of acting out that we can well observe in the treatment of depressives in the transference situation. The patient will exhaust himself in efforts to concentrate on the analyst whatever love is still at his disposal. He will behave in an extremely submissive, masochistic and, at the same time, sadistic way, give himself up to the analyst but expect the impossible in return. He will desire his constant presence and try to blackmail him into a continuous show of omnipotent love, value, and power.

Much depends at this stage, on the analyst's handling of the transference situation. But, as the depressive episode develops, things may get out of hand. The analyst may no longer be able to live up to the patient's expectations. Analyst and patient will be in a trap. The patient will be less and less able to tolerate the analyst's warmth and sympathy, which, failing to elicit an adequate libidinous response, will only increase the disappointment and the hostile claim for a more powerful love. In his fear of a complete breakdown of the object-image, the patient will regress a step further. I emphasized in the first part of the paper that the deserted child prefers an aggressive, strong love-object to its loss. Correspondingly, the patient may now attempt to hold on at least to the reanimated image of an omnipotent, not loving, but punitive, sadistic object. This will manifest itself in the patient's increasing masochistic provocations of the analyst's anger, to a show of aggression, which may bring temporary relief but will actually promote the pathological process.

If the outside world has failed to help the patient in the solution of this conflict, he may turn to his last line of defense: retreat from the object world. The conflict may become fully internalized and a melancholic blatantly psychotic syndrome may develop.

Before we turn to the problem of melancholia, I should like to interpolate that, for reasons of simplification, I have so far deliberately neglected the superego aspects of the depressive conflict.

The melancholic introjection mechanisms seem to represent the last failing attempt at a recovery of the lost original position. What they achieve is at least to restore the powerful object-image by making it a part of the self. What happens is shortly this:

The final escape of the patient from the real object world will, first of all, facilitate a withdrawal of cathexis from the realistic part of the object-representations. Consequently, the object-images will be split up. During the last phase of the conflict the archaic image of a powerful, but punitive, love-object had been built up—as against the image of a weak, bad love-object. This reanimated, inflated image will now be dissolved as a representation in the system ego and will be absorbed by the superego, whereas the deflated worthless object-image merges with the self-representations. Within the self a dangerous schism will develop, which still reflects the patient's effort to rescue the valued object by keeping it protected from his destructive impulses at an unattainable distance from the self. The aggressive forces will accumulate in the superego and cathect the self-image, while the ego gathers the reduced libidinous forces and surrenders to the assault. Thus the patient will succeed in rescuing the powerful love-object but only by a complete deflation or even destruction of the self. The incessant complaints and self-accusations of the melancholic, his exhibition of his helplessness and his moral worthlessness, are both a denial and a confession of guilt: of the crime of having destroyed the valuable love-object. Both indeed tell the truth: the powerful image has collapsed as an object-representation in the ego but it has been reconstituted in the superego.

I may point out once more the difference between these introjection processes and normal or neurotic ego and superego identifications. In normal and in neurotic superego identifications, the object-representations in the ego system are maintained, whereas the melancholic introjection of the "ideal" object-image into the superego goes along with a giving up of the "good" object-representations in the ego and leads to their merging with and a personification of the superego. This is facilitated by the insufficient initial separation between object-image and ego ideal, of which I have talked above. The introjection mechanism in the ego, on the other hand, does not lead to an identification of the ego with the love-object but to a merging of the "worthless" object-image with the image of the self. The ego does not assume any characteristics of the love-object; the self is perceived and is treated by the superego as though it were the deflated love-object.[8]

This metapsychological description and discussion of the problem of depression had of necessity to be one-sided and schematic. I deliberately left out of consideration the corresponding instinctual processes. In the frame of this paper it has seemed to me to be of lesser importance that the melancholic divulges cannibalistic incorporation and anal-sadistic ejection fantasies. All psychotics, schizophrenic or manic-depressive, manifest such deeply regressive id material, which corresponds to the processes that I discussed: the threatening destruction of the object- and self-representations and their restitution by their partial merging. The questions I have tried to explore in this paper are: where, in psychotic depression, these fusions, i.e., introjections, take place from the structural point of view and what they mean with regard to the disintegration of the ego and superego systems. This is why I wished to concentrate on the following issues: the concept of self-represen-

8 Abraham (1911) neglects these differences when he equates the identification with the lost love-object in mourning with the melancholic identification. In his example, the turning gray of his hair after the death of his father, a realistic identification has been achieved.

tations, and its importance for an understanding of the depressive type of identification; the cathectic fluctuations and shifts from self- to object-representations and the reverse, and the fusions with each other; the struggle of the manic-depressive to maintain and recover his position of participation in the power of his love-object; the defense function of the patient's clinging to the real, outside love-object during the depressed period; and, finally, the melancholic symptom formation as an expression of his last failing attempts at restitution of a powerful love-object in the superego.

Naturally, the phases in the development of the depressive conflict and its pathological solution are interwoven and cannot be distinguished so clearly as they are in this description. Even during the free intervals we usually find that the manic-depressive will show more or less continuous vacillations in his mood and efficiency and will try to recover his narcissistic equilibrium once by a clinging to his real love-objects and by claims for support from without and then again by temporary retreats into a pseudo self-sufficiency and attempts to resort to his own superego standards only. This is why I consider it not quite correct to say that during his free intervals he shows compulsive attitudes. It even seems to me that the main difference between the manic-depressive and the compulsive personality is the former's simultaneous or alternate leaning on an idealized love-object and on his own superego, a mixture of pseudo independence and dependency, which true compulsives do not show.

REFERENCES

Abraham, Karl: (1911) Notes on the psycho-analytic investigation and treatment of manic-depressive insanity and allied conditions. In: *Selected Papers on Psycho-Analysis.* London: Hogarth Press, 1927.
—— (1924) A short study of the development of the libido. In: *Selected Papers on Psycho-Analysis.*
Fenichel, Otto: (1939) Über Trophäe und Triumph. *Internationale Zeitschrift für Psychoanalyse und Imago, 24.*
—— (1945) *The Psychoanalytic Theory of Neurosis.* New York: W. W. Norton & Co., Inc.
Freud, Sigm.: (1914) On narcissism: an introduction. In: *Collected Papers, IV.* London: Hogarth Press, 1925.
—— (1917) Mourning and melancholia. In: *Collected Papers, IV.*
Gero, George: (1936) The construction of depression. *International Journal of Psycho-Analysis, 17.*
Hartmann, Heinz: (1950) Comments on the psychoanalytic theory of the ego. In: *The Psychoanalytic Study of the Child, V.* New York: International Universities Press.
Jacobson, Edith: (1943) The oedipus complex in the development of depressive mechanisms. *The Psychoanalytic Quarterly, 12.*
—— (1946) The effect of disappointment on ego and superego formation in normal and depressive development. *Psychoanalytic Review, 33.*
—— (1947) Primary and secondary symptom formation in endogenous depression. Read at the Midwinter Meeting of the American Psychoanalytic Association, New York, December 16, 1947.
Klein, Melanie: (1937) Zur Psychogenese der manisch-depressiven Zustände. *Internationale Zeitschrift für Psychoanalyse und Imago, 23.*
Lewin, Bertram D.: (1950) *The Psychoanalysis of Elation.* New York: W. W. Norton & Co., Inc.
Rado, Sandor: (1928) The problem of melancholia. *International Journal of Psycho-Analysis, 9.*
—— (1951) Psychodynamics of depression from the etiological point of view. *Psychosomatic Medicine, 13.*
Spitz, René A.: (1946) Anaclitic depression. In: *The Psychoanalytic Study of the Child, II.* New York: International Universities Press.
Sterba, Richard: (1947) *Introduction to the Psychoanalytic Theory of the Libido.* New York and Washington: Nervous and Mental Disease Monographs, No. 68.

[83]

"THE DEPRESSIVE POSITION"

Elizabeth Rosenberg Zetzel, M.D.
Boston, Mass.

I WELCOME the opportunity to take part in this panel for a number of reasons. Since returning to this country nearly two years ago, it has been essential for me to reconsider and reassess the views of Mrs. Klein and her followers with which we were so much preoccupied in England—while at the same time comparing and correlating her views with those of workers in this country where much of the recent English work is relatively unknown. The opportunity of organizing and expressing the results of this work is very welcome to me.

To give a full account of Mrs. Klein's views is obviously impossible in a short paper of this type. I shall therefore content myself with a brief enumeration of some of her basic premises and then deal in more detail with the concept of "the depressive position."

It is well known that the most significant feature of Mrs. Klein's work is her attempt to explore and analyze the mental life of the very young infant. The theoretical framework within which the concept of "the depressive position," with which I am mainly concerned in this paper, has developed, rests on certain premises with regard to this early preverbal period which are controversial in many respects. In the first place Mrs. Klein[1] and most of her followers believe that, almost from the outset, and independent of external experience, the infant has innate unconscious knowledge concerning the differences between the sexes and the relationship between the parents. This unconscious knowledge, she suggests, gives rise to a complex fantasy life which plays a decisive role in early development. Mrs. Klein also postulates, and in fact bases many of her most important theories on, the existence of a primary death instinct directed from the outset against the self. It is her contention, too, that processes of introjection and projection constitute the basic mental mechanisms of the first months of life. These three basic cornerstones—first, the existence of innate sexual knowledge; second, the dominant role ascribed to a primary death instinct; and third, the importance attributed to the processes of introjection and projection—determine the individual features of Mrs. Klein's theoretical framework. From the outset, she suggests, the infant's

[1] Cf. *The Psycho-Analysis of Children* (1932) and *Contributions to Psycho-Analysis 1921-1924* (1948). London: Hogarth Press.

[85]

mental life is dominated by conflict between libidinal and aggressive tendencies. In the earliest months these tendencies are related to part objects whose significance is determined by the impulses related to them. There are, in short, good and bad part objects related respectively to loving and aggressive impulses. Owing to the complicated interplay between processes of introjection and projection, these part objects are experienced both as external and as internal. Owing to the unconscious knowledge concerning the sexual relationship between the parents, this complicated interplay between processes of introjection and projection leads very soon to definite fantasies with an oedipal content. These early introjections, derived primarily from the mother's breast, but soon including the father's penis, are regarded by Mrs. Klein as dynamically similar to, if not actually identical with, the definitive superego. In short, Mrs. Klein pushes back the decisive conflicts regarding the oedipus conflict and superego formation to a much earlier period than is generally accepted.

A vitally important aim of all this conflict and fantasy formation is, in her opinion, the decisive and stable introjection of a predominantly good object. The earliest defenses in which good and bad part objects are separated by alternating and variable processes of introjection and projection gradually change in important respects. In the first place, as the infant's grasp of reality develops, the part object becomes a whole object. Concurrently, and also

[86]

largely dependent on reality sense, comes the realization that these good and bad objects are not really
separate, but one and the same. This then brings
about recognition that the love and hate which have
hitherto been directed toward good and bad objects
respectively are in fact directed toward the same object. The infant, that is to say, is faced with the
awareness of his own aggressive destructive fantasies
toward his own loved objects. This recognition then
leads to fear lest his hatred and aggression prove
stronger than his love, which Mrs. Klein calls "depressive fear," and, around the decisive period of
weaning, to his self-reproach and depression concerning the loss of a good object, the breast, which he
attributes primarily to his own destructive impulses.

This very briefly summarizes Mrs. Klein's theory
regarding the background and development of the
depressive position—a subject which I will amplify
later on. At this point I wish to consider first, how
far this concept is dependent on the other premises
and hypotheses I have briefly discussed, and second
whether the various criticisms which have been or
can be made in respect to her work necessarily invalidate the concept of "the depressive position."

With respect to the first point, Mrs. Klein herself
would, I think, maintain that "the depressive position" represents an integral part of her theoretical
framework, and that it cannot be considered out of
its context. In her view, I believe, the significance of
the attainment, and the precariousness, of the good

relationship with a whole good object, whether external or internal, depends on the earlier struggle, which, as you probably know, she considers the basis of paranoid and schizophrenic reactions, with terrifying and aggressive, sadistic and masochistic fantasies concerning the relationship between the parents, the inside of the mother's body, and most important of all the infant's own internal situation resulting from wholesale introjective processes. Finally Mrs. Klein's concept of "the depressive position" is an integral link in her developmental scheme which postulates paranoid and schizoid mechanisms at the earliest level, progressing, as whole object relations develop, to depressive fears and the depressive position, and *followed* by the development of important defenses against the depressive position, of which the most important are the manic defense and the various processes of reparation.

After carefully examining and criticizing her theories, however, I personally do not feel her work to be so closely knit and interdependent that we must either accept or reject *in toto*. With regard to "the depressive position" in particular, I have never felt that the concept of secure object relations as gradually emerging from a struggle with conflicting feelings of love and hate, and a gradual recognition of the identity of the loved and hated object, necessarily rests on Mrs. Klein's reconstruction of violent sadistic fantasies specifically related to the oedipal situation; nor do I feel that the dynamic concept of

[88]

fear of, and reaction to, threatened loss of a good object necessarily implies acceptance of her specific views with regard to the relationship of these early introjections to definitive superego formation.

Since I am concentrating my attention in this paper on the depressive position, I do not wish to spend much time on Mrs. Klein's general theories, important though this would be in a general discussion of her work. I will, however, state my own point of view and will also briefly consider some of the more important criticisms of her work. In the first place, the death instinct is defined and elaborated by Mrs. Klein as an active destructive force originally directed against the self. This does not seem to me a conception in keeping with Freud's formulation, which is itself controversial. On this conception of the death instinct, at best questionable, she has constructed some of her most important formulations— in particular her conception of anxiety. Other important formulations, although *she* would base them on the death instinct, appear equally valid on the premise of aggressive impulses. They do not, that is to say, necessarily, rest on the acceptance of her hypothesis that aggression is originally directed toward the self rather than the outside world.

With regard to Mrs. Klein's other basic theories; her views with regard to early oedipal fantasies, her conception of the importance of introjective and projective processes in the mastery of the basic conflicts between love and hate, and her hypothesis as to

[89]

the early development of the superego, I feel that, in spite of her boldness in approaching the mental life of the young infant, Mrs. Klein's theoretical reconstructions have been marred by too faithful, rather than the reverse, adherence to certain classical analytic hypotheses. To mention only a few: superego formation in the classical view occurs in relation to the oedipus complex. Mrs. Klein in her analytic work finds evidence to suggest the presence of superego-like introjections preceding the genital oedipus complex. Two possibilities are open: first, that the precursors of the superego antedate the oedipus complex; second, that the oedipus complex antedates the genital level. It is the latter alternative Mrs. Klein chooses. Her clinical evidence for this, although clearly illustrating the importance of oedipal fantasies with a predominantly oral or anal coloring, does not, I think, necessarily imply that these pregenital oedipal fantasies must have actually occurred at the time of oral primacy. Here I think her time table is colored by another hypothesis, namely, Abraham's classification of the psychoses in terms of definite libidinal levels. Although certain postulates of her work depend on her abandonment of Abraham's concept of a preambivalent oral phase, Mrs. Klein accepts the hypothesis that schizophrenia and paranoia antedate depression, mania, and the obsessional neurosis. She produces much confirmatory evidence of the archaic qualities of these psychotic mechanisms. This leads her to the conclusion that the fantasies related to these processes must occur in the early months of life. In other words, I feel that Mrs. Klein has entered the field with certain definite analytic preconceptions concerning the psychoses, the oedipus complex, and superego formation, and that these premises have then been applied with some rigidity to her clinical findings. In particular, I feel that this attitude has played an important part in Mrs. Klein's conception of unconscious knowledge and of early oedipal fantasies. In most of these remarks, therefore, I am in substantial agreement with points raised by Robert Waelder in 1937.

Edward Bibring, in a more recent, stimulating critical paper (1947), discusses the premises on which her reconstruction is based and shows quite convincingly the weakness of her theoretical framework. The most important premises, in his opinion, are her conception of innate unconscious knowledge—to which I have already referred—and secondly her conception of activation—which I have not discussed as it seems to me outside the scope of this paper. He concludes,

> If my criticism is valid, all those parts of the developmental reconstruction which are based on these two conceptions are bound to fall with their removal, that is the theoretical structure of the early oedipal fantasies and conflicts compressed into the first six to twelve months of life. . . .[2]

2 Bibring, Edward: The so-called English school of psychoanalysis. *The Psychoanalytic Quarterly, 14,* 1947, pp. 90-91.

Although I am in substantial agreement with Edward Bibring's criticism in this respect, I must point out that it is the specific oedipal content of the reconstruction which seems to me doubtful and unscientific, if for no other reason than that the detailed complexity Mrs. Klein postulates appears to me impracticable and unbiological. I do not, however, feel that this criticism necessarily invalidates the dynamics of the mental processes Mrs. Klein postulates, nor do I think that it undermines her premises regarding the importance of the aggressive instincts from the beginning of life. These are questions to which I shall return.

Glover (1945), in his detailed criticism of Mrs. Klein's view, refers to many of the questions I have raised. He amplifies and illustrates the weaknesses inherent in Mrs. Klein's orientation toward the aggressive instincts; his criticisms of Mrs. Klein's definition of fantasy resembles in many ways Bibring's criticism of the concept of innate knowledge, and appears to me closely related. He also criticizes Mrs. Klein's application of the concepts of fixation and regression. Although he attacks the concept of "the depressive position" as a "closed system"—a criticism I cannot accept—his more important criticisms, like those of Edward Bibring and Robert Waelder, are concerned with Mrs. Klein's reconstruction of the early months of life in terms of the early spontaneous appearance of oedipal fantasies—and the predominant role played in the structure of these fantasies by the aggressive or death instinct which she hypothesizes.

While however I accept these criticisms regarding the theoretical weakness of Mrs. Klein's reconstruction of the early months of life, particularly in respect to oedipal fantasies, I do not feel that this criticism necessarily undermines her conception of "the depressive position." I should therefore now like to turn to our main topic and to discuss in more detail Mrs. Klein's views with regard to the dynamics of mourning and the depressive states. Up to now, that is to say, I have approached this conception on the basis of her reconstructions regarding the growth of object relations. Now I should like to approach the topic from a more orthodox point of view and to compare her views with those of other workers. In this connection I wish first to consider two main topics concerning which theoretical difficulties persist relevant to the dynamic structure of depression. The first concerns the concept of narcissism; the second relates to the process and timing of superego formation.

With respect to narcissism, it is peculiarly difficult to discuss Mrs. Klein's views very adequately. The reason for this difficulty is simple: Mrs. Klein has practically discarded the word narcissism from her vocabulary. In the few references to narcissism in the indices of her two books, almost all are concerned with discussion or quotation of other people's work. At no point does she compare her views regarding

the relationship of libidinal development to ego and
object cathexis with classical theories concerning
narcissistic libido. Although, for example, she refers
briefly to Rado's paper on "The Problem of Melancholia" (1925), she does not amplify the points of
similarity and difference on this particular concept.
I feel this to be a serious omission on her part—all
the more important, because it seems to me that on
this question her work is too significant and important *not* to be brought into a correct orientation in
relation to more orthodox views. Mrs. Klein has, of
course, replaced the concept of narcissism by her emphasis on the importance of internal object relations.
In place of the earlier picture of the infant as an
organism dominated by his need for love and security, as a primary positive need, she puts forward the
concept of an infant struggling from the outset with
the conflict between his loving, positive feelings,
related to situations of satisfaction and fulfillment,
and his aggressive, destructive feelings roused by frustration—a significant amount of which she considers
inevitable in the best feeding situation. Where most
analysts would ascribe excessive need of love and
reassurance (i.e., narcissistic needs) to feelings of
helplessness and inadequacy, Mrs. Klein would suggest that the pathogenicity of such feelings is related
to the feelings of rage, which, occurring at a time
when the infant, it is generally agreed, cannot clearly
distinguish between self and the outside world, is felt

[94]

to be not only destructive to the object but to the self, or its contents, as well.

Owing to Mrs. Klein's neglect of the work of other analysts on the subject of narcissism and the predisposition to depression, it is difficult to assess how far, in fact, her work on this particular subject represents a real departure from accepted views. Leaving aside discussion of the classical papers by Freud (1917) and Abraham (1924), Rado (1925) in particular certainly stresses the intense ambivalence characteristic of the narcissistic struggle in the future melancholic. Gero, too, makes very clear his recognition of this factor when he says,

> His libidinal desires are mixed with aggressive tendencies, the reactions to disappointments. His longing to be loved is too immoderate, too narcissistic; therefore it cannot be gratified. But disappointments activate his equally immoderate aggression which then must be warded off by the ego. The aggression is turned towards the self, towards the introjected object in the ego.[3]

Mrs. Klein, therefore, in spite of her insistence on the one hand on the essential orthodoxy of her views in respect to the most controversial part of her work, to which I have already referred; on the other hand, does not apparently recognize much basic similarity between other parts of her work, in particular with regard to the predisposition to depression, and con-

[3] Gero, George: The construction of depression. *The International Journal of Psycho-Analysis, 17,* 1936, p. 458.

temporary important work by other workers. The reason for this failure appears to me to lie in her apparent abandonment of the concept of narcissism and its replacement by the emphasis laid on processes of introjection and projection and the aggressive instinct. This gives rise to real difficulties of communication and prevents mutual correlation of theoretical orientation, and inevitable exaggeration of what may be at least in part *verbal* differences. My criticism here is not for the moment directed toward what I understand to be the meaning of Mrs. Klein's viewpoint, but toward her failure to express her contribution in terms of its relationship to more orthodox concepts. It is not, that is to say, the fact that she has attempted to dissect and analyze the meaning of narcissism to which I object, but the fact that she has not made it clear either that this is what she is doing, or that she knows she is doing it.

Although I have referred to the recognition by many analysts of the importance of ambivalence in relation to narcissistic needs, it seems to me that this recognition is sometimes more verbal than not, and that there is still a tendency to relate narcissism to a simple apparently unambivalent passive need, without due consideration of the possible relationship between this excessive need and unconscious aggressive tendencies. Bertram D. Lewin (1950), although in a verbal discussion he recognized this relationship, lays great stress in his book on what appear to be mainly positive satisfying experiences in the early months of life, with relatively little reference to the part played by conflict and ambivalence as present from the outset. Mrs. Klein, on the other hand, in abandoning the concept of narcissism has gone to the other extreme. To her, the infant's idyllic experiences appear to be few and far between, and one gets the impression of an infantile mental life dominated by aggressive fantasies and the anxious or depressive reaction to them. Nevertheless I feel that in putting forward the hypothesis that conflict predominates in mental life from the outset, she has made a very important contribution.

The second point I wish to discuss concerns the origin of the superego. Again I will not discuss the classical papers on this subject since the original conception of the superego (i.e., as the heir to the genital oedipus complex) is still accepted by most psychoanalysts. Problems, however, have been discussed— particularly in England, not only by Mrs. Klein and her followers, but also by Ernest Jones, who concluded his paper on "The Origin and Structure of the Super-Ego" with the following statement,

> When, however, we leave these valuable broad generalizations and come to a closer study of some of the problems involved, a number of awkward questions present themselves. There is reason to think that the concept of the super-ego is a nodal point where we may expect all the obscure problems of the Oedipus Complex and narcissism on

the one hand, and hate and sadism on the other, to meet. . . .[4]

The problem, to put it briefly, seems to me essentially this: how do we reconcile the hypothesis that the superego is derived from the genital oedipus complex with the pregenital characteristics of the "depressive superego"? Can we account for these characteristics as *regressive* phenomena ascribable to the pregenital fixations we know to be present in these individuals? Or can we assume that the failure to master pregenital situations has so affected superego formation from the outset that even in relative health, the "depressive superego" is characterized by harsh pregenital features which render the individual particularly vulnerable to any event which by lowering self-esteem will push the pathological superego into melancholic self-reproach? Finally is it not possible that in depressive illness regression takes place to the now generally accepted precursors of the definitive superego which represent the introjection and identifications of the pregenital period?

The problem before us here, too, is the explanation not only of the oral, pregenital nature, of the "depressive superego," but also of the generally recognized oral features found in the analysis of the oedipal situation itself in these patients. It is generally agreed—for I think the emphasis given this subject in all discussions of the subject points to a

4 *Collected Papers on Psycho-Analysis*, 4th edition. London: Baillière, Tindall & Cox, 1937, p. 188.

consensus of opinion—that the question of superego formation is a crucial point in this problem.

I should like at this point to recapitulate Mrs. Klein's views on this problem. She gives, briefly, the following answers: the archaic pregenital nature of the superego in these patients points to the possibility that the definitive superego has antecedents, structurally comparable, which are formed at pregenital levels. In melancholic individuals, because of failure to master the conflicts of this period, superego structure retains these archaic characteristics which reappear in the regression of melancholic illness. The presence of oedipal fantasies of a predominantly oral nature she would explain not as a regressive phenomenon attributable to the disease process, but as illustrating the presence of early oedipal fantasies of a predominantly oral and sadistic nature—in the early months of life.

In discussing the same basic problem, Edith Jacobson comes to a different conclusion. In her opinion, to quote,

the superego is a compound of oedipus strivings and prohibitions as well as a compromise with regard to infantile narcissistic desires. It denies the child the desired parental omnipotence, yet sets up the God image within the ego. . . . This is accomplished by the regressive reanimation of originally omnipotent parental images.[5]

5 Jacobson, Edith: The effect of disappointment on ego and superego formation in normal and depressive patients. *The Psychoanalytic Review, 33,* 1946, p. 134.

In other words, the archaic nature of the "depressive superego" does not necessarily point to pregenital superego functions. It is rather attributable to regressive processes, precipitated by disappointment at the oedipal level, which reanimate the introjections of an earlier period. It is relevant to note here Edith Jacobson's assumption that early pregenital parental introjections, however activated, play a decisive part in superego formation. It is also worth noting that she too raises the possibility of premature superego formation in the future depressive.

To Edith Jacobson, an oedipal situation complicated by severe disappointment in both parents occurring in an individual of depressive predisposition may be decisive both for superego formation and for the probability of future depressive illness. I should like to take this opportunity of amplifying my discussion of Mrs. Klein's views by comparing them with Edith Jacobson's. Mrs. Klein would, I think, agree in accepting the importance of disappointment in the parents at this critical period: she would, however, be concerned in elucidating the *significance* to the child of this disappointment in the light of its own fantasies and fears. Edith Jacobson for example lays great stress on the pathogenic significance of devalued, useless parents—compared with that of powerful parents—whether for good or evil. She postulates an identification with these devalued useless parents, leading to diminution of the ego and the sense of worthlessness so characteristic of the depressive. She would, however, I think regard the precipitating event in this pathogenic chain of events as emanating from some real failure on the part of the parents. Mrs. Klein, on the other hand, while accepting the real disappointment, would relate its pathogenic effect to the mental state of the child at the time of the disappointment in the specific sense that she would attribute the child's depressive reaction to its feeling of guilt and responsibility for the parent's failure. The devalued parents, which both Edith Jacobson and Mrs. Klein agree to be introjected into the ego would, according to Mrs. Klein's point of view, represent the damaged or destroyed parents, or combined parental figure; the child, in short, attributing the parental disappointment to its own aggression and hostility.

In considering these problems concerning the structure of melancholia and its relation to the nature of narcissism and to early superego formation, I have so far discussed some of the more important work on the subject and compared in certain respects Mrs. Klein's views with those of other workers. So far, however, I have been concerned mainly with the structure and meaning of pathological depression and have mainly shown the type of problem which Mrs. Klein is attempting to solve. I have not as yet discussed in any detail the most controversial aspect of Mrs. Klein's views on depression: namely, her concept of "the depressive position" as a normal phenomena in infantile life. To do this I must once more return to the question of mourning and melancholia. Mrs. Klein in her work on this subject has made two significant suggestions. In the first place she has suggested that the differences between mourning and melancholia, although decisive for the mental health of the individual, are not as great as has sometimes been suggested. In her extremely interesting description of the experience of a normal mourner she illustrates particularly by dream analysis, how in a brief, modified form which is eventually overcome by healthy defenses and reparative processes, the mental state of the mourner is comparable in every respect with that of the melancholic. There is, unconsciously, definite evidence of self-reproachful processes, guilt with regard to the death of the lost love object, devaluation of the self. There is, too, a sense of triumph with subsequent guilt which is clearly related to aggressive fantasies. Gradually, however, the normal mourner is able to set up within himself a predominantly positive introjection of the lost love object, and when this is accomplished the work of mourning is more or less complete. Mrs. Klein also gives a good deal of material illustrating how the real external loss revives or reactivates in the individual his earlier struggles of a similar nature, most of which appeared referable to the earliest relation with the mother. In the normal mourner that is to say, the real object loss revives this decisive previous struggle. In individuals who have made an early satisfactory solution with subsequent good object relationships, mourning is successfully accomplished. In others where this early struggle resulted in comparative failure and difficulties in achieving and maintaining good object relationships, the reaction to loss will approach more or less closely a clinical depression.

With regard to Mrs. Klein's formulations regarding pathological conditions, in particular the more severe depressive illnesses, where the part played by real object loss is obscure and unrecognized, I must express considerable reserve. Her adult patients, for the most part, appear to be severe neurotics, personality problems, and examples of typical neurotic depression. I do not personally feel that the differences between these cases and the more severe patients seen in hospitals are straightforward or predominantly quantitative. I believe, in this respect, that Mrs. Klein underestimates the importance both of constitutional factors and of the complexity of the whole process of maturation. This view seems to be in accordance with Edward Bibring's emphasis on the part played by complicating factors in determining the different clinical manifestations of depression. Edward Bibring,[6] however, has also emphasized the fundamental unity of the basic feelings of depression. He showed that in spite of the wide range between for example mild sadness, mourning, and feelings of disinterest, many of which are within the scope of normal experience, and the various pathol-

[6] See pp. 13-48.

ogical conditions in which depression is a presenting symptom, there is a basic unity of the depressive process. With this point of view, Mrs. Klein would be in agreement, although her conception of the dynamics of these basic feelings differs in important respects from his.

This unitary conception of depression, however, makes it essential to be very clear as to Mrs. Klein's meaning when she postulates the existence of depressive tendencies as a normal phenomenon of infantile life. It is, in short, particularly important to ascertain whether, in talking of "the infantile depressive position," she is comparing the infant with the adult melancholic or with the normal mourner. In my opinion, some of the objections to her conception arise from a misunderstanding of this crucial point. Granted that there are accepted resemblances between mourning and melancholia, the crucial differences between them must always be borne in mind. Mourning, however painful, is, no matter how much its dynamic unconscious structure resembles that of pathogenic illness, a normal human experience which few of us escape. I do not personally feel that anyone who has either undergone this experience with psychological insight into his own mental state or who has had an opportunity of analyzing someone immediately after bereavment could fail to confirm much that Mrs. Klein says about the ambivalent reactions related to the introjection of the lost love object, and, most important from our point

[104]

of view, about the revival of primitive feelings of conflict and dependence on the mother. Mrs. Klein, in postulating the conception of an early "depressive position" as crucial, not only in relation to the reaction to real object loss, but for the development of good object relations throughout life, is, I think, referring to the manner in which the weaning process constitutes a real object loss. She is offering the hypothesis that the attainment of a predominantly positive object relationship prior to this first object loss is crucial for future development. The infant, that is to say, during the weaning process must come to terms with a real object loss—i.e., the breast or its substitute. This is the basis for the concept of a "depressive position." Now this loss, like the real losses of later life, is an inevitable event in human development and one which, it is generally accepted, is of great emotional significance for the child. What determines its successful or unsuccessful outcome? And what is the significance of this conflict for future mental health with particular reference to depression? It is in our answers to these questions that the significance of Mrs. Klein's approach becomes clear. Mrs. Klein suggests that—just as with the adult mourner—it is the successful introjection of a predominantly good object which is the goal. Where, however, the relatively greater strength of the aggressive impulses prevents this occurrence the introjected good object is felt to be lost, and is, typically, replaced by the hostile damaged or destroyed ob-

[105]

jects which so closely resemble the devalued parents described by Edith Jacobson. In between these two extremes occur all the infinite variations in object relationship that are so familiar to all of us.

Not only psychoanalysts but anthropologists, psychologists, and pediatricians, have in recent years stressed with increasing vigor the importance of the early mother-child relationship for the successful development of the human infant. There are, of course, differences of opinion as to how far either success on the one hand, or failure on the other, play a decisive role in the later crucial emotional struggles of childhood. In spite, however, of the real difficulties of proving in our analytic work how far our reconstructions of preverbal mental life are valid, I think we would all agree as to the importance of these experiences of the early months in providing or not providing a foundation of security and positive feeling as the basis for future object relationships. Most of the work on this subject has stressed the infant's basic need—indeed inherent right—to the security which appears to be such a basic requirement. That undue frustration produces a variety of pathological developments is also generally accepted.

Spitz (1946), in his interesting and important contributions to the psychopathology of infancy, has clearly demonstrated the overt depressive states precipitated in infants forcibly separated from their mothers during the second six months of life. In these cases, to the inevitable struggle over the loss of the breast was added the concurrent loss of the mother as a whole—a situation differing decisively from that of the normal infant, where, as Mrs. Klein points out, "The whole situation and the defences of the baby who obtains reassurance over and over again in the love of the mother, differ greatly from those in the adult melancholic."[7] The fact that loss of the mother during this decisive period produces actual clinical depression seems to me evidence in favor of the depressive vulnerability of the infant at this point. Other observers, too, have noted the decisive change in the babies' relationship to the mother at or about six months, and they agree as to the special vulnerability of the baby to separation from its mother at the time when he comes to know her as a whole person.

Edward Bibring[8] in his paper suggests that the source or anlage of depressive symptoms may be sought in the feelings of helplessness of the infant in the face of frustration. I think it possible that he, too, might be inclined to agree that the critical period for this experience is related to the emergence of a whole object relationship—where the need and desire are first related to a specific individual, the mother. The decisive problem for us, however, is to decide how far this recognized dependence of the infant on security and gratification imply that re-

[7] Klein, Melanie: The psycho-genesis of manic-depressive states. *Contributions to Psycho-Analysis 1921-1945*. London: Hogarth Press, 1948, p. 307.

[8] See pp. 13-48.

actions of helplessness and rage constitute a response to a specific traumatic experience of frustration and rejection on the part of the mother. This I believe to be implicit in most orthodox opinions. The alternative proposed by Mrs. Klein is that the degree of depressive anxiety aroused by greater or less external frustration will depend not only on the environmental situation but on the infant's anxieties regarding his own aggressive tendencies. Let us, for the sake of simplification, accept for the moment the proposition that at or around the time of weaning, the infant has developed a real enough object relationship with its mother to feel helpless, frightened or depressed at her threatened or actual loss. Do we explain this reaction as a simple maturation phenomenon—i.e., as a reaction which must inevitably occur when the infant comes to know his mother and his own dependence on her for gratification? Or do we, on the other hand, believe that in addition to these maturation processes, there has already been a gradual psychological development from part to whole object relationships and that during this period, characterized by confusion between outer and inner worlds and conflict between love and hate, introjective and projective processes have played an important part? In other words, how far do we believe with Mrs. Klein that the infant during the early sucking period believes or fears that the absent breast is gone because it is inside him?

Obviously we are here in the realm of reconstruction since up to the present no scientific proof has been possible. With regard to observations on young infants I have mentioned some suggestive evidence. Most of our information, however, is derived—as I think it must be—from our analytic work. To me, and I think to many British-trained analysts who have been stimulated by Mrs. Klein's work but who have not joined her followers, her conception of the growth of object relationships in an ambivalent setting is her most valuable contribution. There is much clinical material in keeping with the concept that the struggle between love and hate leads to depressive fears lest the hating impulses prove the stronger. One common analytic example of the type of material I have in mind is concerned with the struggle to maintain a good object relationship in the transference situation in spite of negative feelings often aroused by the analyst's absence or lateness— most typically of all, perhaps, in connection with the temporary breaks during vacation periods. The importance of this material, from the point of view of this panel, is not in its rarity but in its ubiquity. The intensity of these reactions varies all the way from a true, though temporary, depression to feelings of mild anxiety where the depressive content only reveals itself in dreams. The decisive factor in determining the quality and pathogenicity of these reactions clearly relates to the degree to which the individual is capable of tolerating his own recognition of ambivalence without feeling too anxious lest his hate prove stronger than his love. In more disturbed patients, in particular in those with under-lying, often unconscious depressive features, the in-ability to tolerate this conflict is over and over again demonstrated by, for example, excessively positive feelings expressed during analytic sessions, with a tendency to react to the analyst's absence even over week ends with fears lest he is or about to be maimed or destroyed. That this material is related to early feeding situations has been strongly suggested in cer-tain cases both by the oral content of the material and by a known history of early feeding problems with a lifelong ambivalence of object relationships.

How far, however, can we assume that these am-bivalent reactions to frustration and loss in either child or adult patients must be regarded as partial or complete repetitions of earlier reactions? A similar and crucial scientific question also remains as to how far we are justified in assuming that material which appears to be deepest, both in difficulty of access and in its primitive archaic structure, is necessarily earliest from the developmental point of view? It is certain that Mrs. Klein has pushed both these premises to their utmost limits and beyond the point where any satisfactory method of validation has yet been discovered. Nevertheless, I wish to stress once more that I do not believe that either Mrs. Klein's theoretical framework, or her specific reconstructions regarding the content of infantile fantasies, consti-tute her main or most significant contribution to analytic thought. These formulations I regard as her attempts to verbalize material which is fundamentally preverbal in nature—an attempt which, as I stated before, is colored by her efforts to couch her formulations within the framework of more or less orthodox analytic hypotheses.

A possible explanation is that vague and often diffuse bodily and emotional experiences related to the parents, which, in the early months of life, may well enter into and color the later oedipal situation in important respects, are treated as if these later conflicts had already been present at the earlier period. This I believe happens because during analysis and probably particularly during the analysis of children at or around the crucial oedipal period, the material presents itself as if the nursing infant had experienced the fantasies expressed so clearly by the four- or five-year-old. The material, that is to say, is true: it is not, however, necessarily correct in timing owing to the retrospective oedipal interpretation of earlier experiences.

The decisive question, however, as I see it, concerns the nature and origin of mental conflict in the human infant. At first glance Mrs. Klein's conception of the aggressive instincts raises many questions from a biological and common-sense point of view. The whole science of psychoanalysis, however, derives from what might well be called the unbiological and uncommon-sensical nature of the human being. It seems to me a hypothesis worth very full examination

—namely, that the combination of excessive helplessness with the capacity for more or less distinct awareness of this situation long before the development of any effective mode of reaction—may well result in the early appearance, not only of aggressive impulses, which are well recognized, but also of psychological attempts to explain experience in the light of these conflicting emotions: i.e., fantasies, or perhaps better the preverbal precursors of fantasies. Moreover, we have much analytic experience to suggest that along with these feelings of helplessness there exist important and significant feelings of omnipotence, which refer not only to the positive power to fantasy the wished-for breast, for example, but also negative convictions that the absence itself has been brought about by an omnipotent destructive impulse.

In considering Mrs. Klein's views I have tried as far as possible to separate her theoretical framework, which is often obscure and in many respects controversial, from what appear to me the more significant aspects of her approach to the problem of depression in relation to the development of object relations and early mental conflict. Here I feel that although her point of view raises a number of vitally important issues—in particular concerning the nature of narcissism, the role of the aggressive instincts, and the development of the superego—much of her work need not necessarily imply any important departure from orthodox analytic views. Finally with regard to the concept of "the depressive position," I feel that more than anything else the term is unfortunate, since it seems to imply more far-reaching implications of infantile psychosis than is in fact the case. As suggested, there seems to me a good deal of work to substantiate her conception that the achievement of a whole object relationship is accompanied by anxiety and a definite and specific vulnerability to depression in the event of object loss. In this sense, therefore, the concept of "the depressive position"— under some more suitable name (I have for example suggested the term "depressive vulnerability")—may well prove a concept of considerable importance in our growing knowledge of the development of object relations.

To sum up: in this paper I have approached Mrs. Klein's concept of "the depressive position" from two points of view. In the first place, I described her general theoretical orientation with special reference to the development of "the depressive position." I then considered how far this concept was separable from the whole context of her theories and whether or not criticism directed against these theories necessarily included "the depressive position." In the second place, I have attempted to approach the subject by discussing some important views on the subject of depression in comparison with Mrs. Klein's. Finally I have tried to consider the significance of her concept of "the depressive position" with particular reference to normal mourning. For reasons of brevity I have not discussed many important aspects of her work—in particular her conception of mania and of the processes of reparation.

To conclude: it may seem that by whittling down and pruning Mrs. Klein's work in this connection, I have left relatively little that is objectionable, but also, since after all other workers—Rado, Gero, Jacobson, to mention only a few—have also stressed the significance of ambivalent struggles in early childhood in relation to depression, little that is important or individual. My wish, however, in this paper has been to evaluate to the best of my ability the scientific validity of Mrs. Klein's views in the light of our present state of knowledge. It is always essential in any science, but perhaps particularly in our own, to remember to distingush between that which we believe to be true and which, as far as our powers of validation go, we feel proved to be true, and that which offers suggestive and fruitful hypotheses which may be true but which must so far be considered unproved.

Mrs. Klein's views, although they offer dynamic and stimulating hypotheses, belong to the latter category. I am safe in saying that few who have worked with her have failed to be impressed by her immediacy of insight into the deeper levels of the unconscious mind. Her interpretations of the dreams, fantasies, and the associations of numerous patients, have resulted in a considerable body of evidence regarding the existence and importance of many of the conflicts she hypothesizes. Nevertheless there is a

[114]

considerable step between recognizing and interpreting specific unconscious material, and constructing a theoretical reconstruction with far-reaching implications. Mrs. Klein's theoretical framework is not only based on her clinical findings but on her specific premises regarding the basic instincts and archaic mental processes. In so far, therefore, as these premises are not regarded as proved, her theoretical framework cannot be considered to rest on a sound basis. It would, however, be unfortunate for the development of psychoanalysis, if Mrs. Klein's controversial theoretical approach, and occasional verbal obscurity, should lead us to forget the importance and significance of her dynamic approach to the problems of early infantile development.

BIBLIOGRAPHY

Abraham, Karl: (1924) A short study of the development of the libido. In: *Selected Papers on Psycho-Analysis*. London: Hogarth Press, 1942.

Bibring, Edward: (1947) The so-called English school of psychoanalysis. *The Psychoanalytic Quarterly, 16*.

Freud, Sigmund: (1914) On Narcissism: an introduction. In: *Collected Papers, IV*. London: Hogarth Press, 1925.

—— (1915) Mourning and melancholia. In: *Collected Papers, IV*.

Gero, George: (1936) The construction of depression. *International Journal of Psycho-Analysis, 17*.

Glover, Edward: (1945) Examination of the Klein system of child psychology. In: *The Psychoanalytic Study of the Child, I*. New York: International Universities Press.

Jacobson, Edith: (1946) The effect of disappointment on ego and super-ego formation in normal and depressive development. *The Psychoanalytic Review, 33*.

Jones, Ernest: (1937) The origin and the structure of the superego. In: *Collected Papers on Psycho-Analysis*, 4th edition. London: Bailliere, Tindall & Cox.

Klein, Melanie: (1935) Contribution to the psycho-genesis of the manic-depressive states. In: *Contributions to Psycho-Analysis 1921-1945*. London: Hogarth Press, 1948.

—— (1940) Mourning, its relation to manic-depressive states. In: *Contributions to Psycho-Analysis 1921-1945*.

Lewin, Bertram D.: (1950) *The Psychoanalysis of Elation*. New York: W. W. Norton & Company, Inc.

Rado, Sandor: (1925) The problem of melancholia. *International Journal of Psycho-Analysis, 9*.

Spitz, René A.: (1946) Anaclitic depression. In: *The Psychoanalytic Study of the Child, II*. New York: International Universities Press.

Waelder, Robert: (1937) The problem of the genesis of psychical conflict in earliest infancy. *International Journal of Psycho-Analysis, 18*.

AN EQUIVALENT OF DEPRESSION: ANOREXIA

GEORGE GERO, M.D.
New York, N. Y.

THE TITLE of this paper needs elucidation; and equivalent of depression designates a neurotic condition which shows many of the essential features of genuine chronic depression, yet with differences in the symptomatology. Such a comparative study of two closely related nosological groups is carried out in the hope of clarifying some problems of symptom formation.

I have selected a case of severe anorexia as a starting point for my investigation because the impact of conflicts that involve the oral drives is already evident in the choice of symptom. Clinical experience shows that the same or similar conflicts are at work in depressions too. Yet, although conflicts concerning food intake are frequent enough in depressions, they do not always result in anorexia.

I shall present some fragments from a long and

[117]

complicated case history. A female patient came to me, with a history of long-standing neurotic suffering, consisting mainly of eating difficulties and severe phobic symptoms, which progressively curtailed her social life. Habitually underweight at times of special emotional stress, she suffered an exacerbation of her anorexia and looked uncannily haggard, almost skeleton-like. Her symptom improved during analysis, but it did not disappear entirely. Just because of this severity and stubborn persistence of the symptom, it was possible for me to gain deeper insight into its mechanism. Eating was a grave and grim struggle in the life of this patient, even the thought of food at times being repugnant. At other times her revulsion from food would overcome her in the course of a meal, and might result in pain and vomiting. At such times the food appeared to her as dangerous, representing a terrible threat: something which could destroy her. The concern about food was paralleled by the concern about her body, about her thinness. At a time when the prevailing ideal of beauty for women demanded extreme slimness, and a few extra pounds would spell disaster for others, the day's mood was set for this patient if, while dressing, she would discover that her skirt was too loose around her waist. She would then feel deeply depressed, considering herself too childlike and so thin as to be almost without a body. In conspicuous contrast to her revulsion against food were her repeated dreams of feasts, in which she ate with uninhibited greed, ingesting great amounts of food. During certain phases in analysis the cannibal impulses appeared openly in her dreams, e.g., she was eating a chicken which changed into a baby; or the phallic and coprophagic impulses broke through, e.g., she dreamed that she was picking celery from a garbage can and eating it greedily.

This patient was extremely dissatisfied with her life. Her desire for a feminine destiny was unfulfilled. She was unmarried and she was unable to establish relationships with men. She was successful as a business woman, and appreciated by her numerous friends. But in spite of such partial exception she lived in a deep neurotic isolation and loneliness. Consequently the sessions in analysis were filled with never-ending, repetitious complaints about the misery of her life. It was inconceivable, she constantly said, that any man could love her; it was inconceivable that she could live a normal life. While she was right about the depth of the neurotic suffering which became her destiny, her depressive complaints had the typical flavor of self-flagellation. The intensity with which she dwelt upon her suffering, her self-indulgence in this suffering was obviously masochistic. She was especially worried about her symptoms, her eating difficulties, and the tendency to develop dizziness in situations that stirred up her unconscious sexual fantasies or those in which she also experienced unconscious sexual temptation. Eating became the symbol for all her suffering and assumed magic significance in her mind; if only she could eat, then everything would clear up for her. Clearly, the greater the magic significance of food, the greater became her eating disturbance.

From an external point of view her childhood was not unusual. She had good, loving parents, who cared for their children. Her mother undoubtedly wanted sons rather than daughters, and as my patient was the second child and the second daughter, her mother was disappointed and probably conveyed her disappointment to my patient. Between mother and daughter developed a mutually reinforcing hostility: my patient reacted to the feeling of not being loved with great hostility, which increased the mother's disappointment, resulting in an attitude of maternal martyrdom, as if to indicate "You see, whatever I do for you is no use. You are and will remain an ungrateful child."

Her history was clear as far back as to her fifth year of life. At this point her mother gave birth to a boy, the son for whom she had longed so ardently. My patient was then at the peak of her oedipal yearnings and conflicts. Concomitantly she went through a period of intensive masturbatory activities. While the memory of the mother's pregnancy was repressed, some details from the delivery were retained. She peeped through the keyhole of the bathroom and saw the doctor's bloody instruments. She also heard her mother moaning and saw her in bed, pale and with a suffering expression on her face.

Shortly after the brother's birth, her eating difficulties started. They were not as severe then as at the
time of her analysis, but severe enough to worry her
parents. She was taken to a doctor, who found her
anemic and prescribed iron, which did not help very
much. Clearly it was not this traumatic event itself
which set forth the foundation for the neurosis, but
the impact upon the drives, fantasies and corresponding anxieties of the patient.

All the leading themes of this decisive period of
her childhood were expressed in her masturbatory
fantasies, and in turn, these fantasies revealed the
driving forces of her neurosis. She had two sets of
fantasies: an early one depicted her mother alone,
her face expressing sexual excitement, her body ap-
pearing in a lascivious pose, and a later adolescent
version of this. In the course of her analysis the hidden content of this early fantasy became apparent:
her mother was masturbating. This fantasy filled her
with rage—rage against the mother. Her own masturbation, which accompanied the fantasy, was carried out as an attack against the mother. She would
have to tell herself, "I have to do this because of you,
I have to be bad, because you are bad," and the
masturbatory action, which consisted in rubbing and
pulling the clitoris, was an attack directed against
her own body and her mother's body simultaneously.
The later set of fantasies crystallized definitely probably first during adolescence. In these fantasies the
mother no longer appeared and the patient herself

played the leading role. She was a low, bad girl, who by her lascivious behavior provoked one or two men to attack her sexually. It took a long time in her analysis before the nature of this "attack" could be verbalized. Finally, it turned out that the attack consisted in these men pulling at her clitoris vigorously and brutally. This was performed as if it were some kind of punishment which they executed, a punishment which nevertheless gave her a unique pleasure.

These fantasies and the attendant act of masturbation filled her with shame and horror. The strongest resistance had to be overcome before she could verbalize the fantasy. But the resistance did not cease with the verbalization of the fantasy. The source of greatest resistance remained that the analysis would lead to a revival of her masturbatory urge. She considered it as a triumph that she was successful in fighting it off. Following the intensive masturbatory period of her childhood she developed the idea that her genital organs, more specifically the clitoris, were disfigured and enlarged as a result of masturbation. This fear haunted her constantly and was the secret source of her apprehension of being rejected by men. In her analysis when masturbatory excitement was stirred up, she reacted in a specially characteristic way peculiar to her, namely, primarily with bodily sensations. For example, when the masochistic wish to be attacked came near to consciousness, she felt an intense pain in her genital region. She reacted in the same way when the memories of her mother's delivery were analyzed. Again an intense pain in the genital region indicated the masochistic identification with her mother.

This patient showed identical trends in her bodily reaction. The same spastic rebellion that was manifested by her oesophagus and stomach against food, she produced vaginally during intercourse. Contraction of the vagina at the beginning of the intercourse and not at the climax, indicated her refusal to accept the penetration by her partner's penis with receptive feminine pleasure. She acted as if to keep the penis out or to bite it off.

The rich material of the analysis seemed to show that eating represented for the patient the condensation of sexual drives and fantasies in which her whole sexuality was invested. The most important of the condensations was the equation between eating and femininity. If one could eat, one became "big," feminine. One would have the big and powerful body of the mother. Eating from this point of view became a magic act, the means through which one regained not only the lost penis, but possibly also the mother's magic ability to grow things inside her body, and in this fantasy the penis was replaced by babies. Eating also meant feminine attraction, meant the mother's power over the father, her ability to elicit the father's love. But being loved by the father meant for my patient the dangers which, according to her fantasies, were concomitant with femininity. The discovery of the anatomical sex difference, the observations at the birth of the brother, the observations of parental intercourse, were joined in a grandiose condensation in which the process of eating expressed all these fantasies. To repeat, eating meant to become a woman and suffer masochistically the feminine destiny. The intensity of the masochistic forces caused her to repeat again and again the struggle against her drives and fantasies. The decisive moment for the symptom formation of the anorexia was the disposition of the organism to express psychological conflicts in a somatic way.

The subject of this paper is not so much anorexia in itself, as a comparative study between anorexia and depression. Therefore I shall not review the recent literature on this subject. I wish to mention only the valuable papers on this subject by Lorand (1943), K. Eissler (1943), and Sylvester (1945). I note areas of agreement, especially between Lorand's views and the interpretation of the case which I have just presented.

The present state of psychoanalytic views on depression is the subject of this panel and the analysts with new viewpoints on depression have given accounts of their work. In preparing my contribution I was able to utilize only what was published already in the literature. Edith Jacobson's (1946) work deals with what she calls early disappointment and the impact on the superego formation. Edward Bibring,[1] whose paper appears as part of this panel,

[1] See this Volume, pp. 13-48.

stresses that the feeling of helplessness in bringing back the lost object is the essence of the depressive reaction. I am under the impression from hearing his discussions that his emphasis is one with which I am in essential accord from my own observations.

Let me review the mechanism of the depression in my patient. Her deep sadness really was based on her feeling that she cannot be loved. In her analysis the complicated structure of this attitude became apparent. She was afraid that she could not be loved by a man, that no man could accept her. It turned out that this fear of rejection was a defense, for it helped her to avoid what to her seemed the terrible dangers of sexual relations with men. Time and again in her transference she went through a characteristic cycle, when she shifted over to the analyst her positive oedipal longings. When she wanted to be loved by me but after a short period of feeling happy and alive, she would dip into a deep depression. But interestingly, in this depressed mood she was not concerned, as one would have expected, about the hopelessness of obtaining gratification of her longings. In other words, she was not grieving for the lost love object, but she grieved about her poor self. Her depressive complaints revolved around herself and particularly about her body, about the ugliness of her body. And while she was putting so much emphasis on her sorrow and the fact that she could not be loved, it was quite obvious that she herself was not able to love; that she was not even able to be

[125]

interested in anybody apart from herself. In this state any sexual longing, or even sexual feeling disappeared. What she repeated was clearly the breaking down of her oedipal longing for her father and the shifting from the grief caused by this loss to the loss of the penis. The oedipal nature of her dissatisfaction with her body was quite clearly demonstrated by the fact that the negative accent of her own body image was contrasted with the body image of her mother. She expressed despair that she could not develop the big full body of a woman and that she was doomed to remain little and childlike. At the same time it was obvious that she could not accept a feminine body. What she wanted, was a magic quality which she attributed to her mother, the ability to grow things in her body. While she was wishing for this magic quality, she felt utter disgust toward the motherly contours of the feminine body. Since early childhood the big belly of her mother had represented for her the quintessence of ugliness. The body image of the mother was split into two contradictory aspects: from the one point of view it represented the powerful body with the magic quality, while from the other point it appeared as destroyed bloody mess. Her oedipal longings were doomed to frustration because she could not find a way out of the dilemma presented to her by the contradictory images of the mother's body. Her masochistic longings drove her toward what she depicted as the painful and feminine destiny, yet she was forced to flee from these longings into a narcissistic retreat and isolation. The mechanism of depression, in this case at least, can be fully understood in the frame of the oedipus situation.[2]

Here I should like to discuss the interrelation of the patient's oral conflicts and oedipal problems and use the material for theoretical reflections. During the analysis the oral drives of this patient crystallized very impressively. The cannibalistic impulses, as mentioned, often appeared quite openly. In her sexual fantasies, when she imagined herself kissing a man, she felt an impulse to bite her imaginary partner, to tear at him with her teeth. Her oral drives appeared in manifold expressions of the transference. Sometimes during the sessions she expressed the desire to take me in, the whole of me—that is, she wanted to eat me up. This impulse, she felt, was the expression of love. In contrast to this, which might be called the friendly wish for total incorporation, she experienced angry, hostile, tearing and biting impulses, at first with a vague intention but later, after overcoming great resistance, directed against the penis. It was interesting to follow up in which context the change from the friendly to the hostile oral impulses occurred in her. In the course of analysis it was possible to localize the turning point exactly. The origin of this change was reflected in the masturbatory fantasy; the tearing and biting impulse against the man's penis appeared as a reaction against her own masochistic wish that a man should

[2] See Gero (1936).

tear at her genitalia. These observations which I present here in a condensed form seem to me to lead to a rather significant conclusion; namely, that we must correct, at least at one point, Abraham's view of the pathognomic significance of the oral fixation points. Abraham (1924), as you will recall, held the view that the point in the development of the oral drives at which fixation occurs is of great significance for the etiology of the depression. According to him, the point of fixation of the depression is characteristically in the early cannibalistic phase, a phase which he conceived of as having the aim to destroy the object. Cases such as mine, and other clinical observations as well, disprove this point.

First, we see that the different aspects of orality coexist in the same individual, or that oral drives enter into the formation of different drive patterns in the same individual; further that the impulse of total incorporation—or, to use a more plastic phrase, the wish to eat up the object—is not necessarily a hostile one, a destructive wish, but the expression of the libidinal need to merge with the object. We see further that the difference between total and partial incorporation does not have the sharp distinctive pathognomic significance, which Abraham attributed to it. We cannot agree that the need for total incorporation is in itself a sign of the severity of the pathological process, as Abraham believed it to be. We must rather view the diversity of oral drives as originating from a common root, i.e., the nursing situation, as B. D. Lewin (1950) describes it, an inherited pattern with a certain flexibility influenced by the vicissitudes of life history. R. A. Spitz's (1946) observations on infants, as far as I know, do not furnish evidence of increased biting impulses as a symptom of early depression. Some depressive patients learn from their mothers that they bit while at the breast, of others no such misdeeds were recorded. My anorexia patient, according to her mother, was a docile baby, never given to biting. She was nursed until she was a year old and was then weaned abruptly. She once overheard a conversation between her mother and a friend. The mother was describing how she weaned her children by painting her breasts and applying some unpleasant-tasting salve to the nipples. My patient was outraged on learning this, the more so because she thought that she could detect in her mother's voice an almost lascivious quality, a quality she had observed when sexual allusions were made among adults. I shall return later to the evaluation of the early oral history of my patient.

At this point it is desirable to stress the remarkable fact that this patient in whom cannibalistic impulses were so strongly emphasized, did not show any signs of increased biting tendencies in her infancy. Her oral impulses and fantasies appeared in patterns which represented purely libidinal or sadistic tendencies, and in the course of analysis one could study the constellation in which a change of the drive pattern took place. Her mother's body, chiefly her belly, was the target of oral-sadistic impulses. The aim was to tear out something, babies, or the penis. No doubt, the mother's body was the aim of purely libidinal impulses, too, the desire for the breast, since a merging with the big, protecting body of the mother played an important role in her emotional life. Her oral impulses in regard to her father's penis were equally ambivalent. To bite off the penis could appear as the expression of rage and hostility, or just as well, as an expression of a strange kind of love, and subjectively she could very well differentiate between a friendly incorporative wish and an impulse for an oral attack.

Before further discussion of the impact of oral conflicts in the etiology of depression, some general remarks are in order. The advantage of our present position in psychoanalysis lies in the great wealth of observations we have at our disposal. This advantage enables us to make finer differentiations and work out operational concepts of greater plasticity. On the other hand, there is danger in this situation, for we do not always realize that we are talking about different phenomena and arrive at theories which contradict each other. Such contradictions are not always necessarily based on real differences in our theoretical positions.

To come back to the problem confronting us now: theoretical conclusions will obviously depend on the type of cases of which we are thinking. Freud (1917) in his classical study "Mourning and Melancholia," had the severe melancholic cases in mind, when he based his interpretation on the mechanism of the self-reproaches. Abraham's cases belonged to the manic-depressive group. Some of the recent theories on depression are based, so it seems to me, on a different clinical group, on the chronic neurotic depression, or on a corresponding character disturbance, the depressive character. My case of anorexia belongs in this latter category. But even in the same type of depression different aspects of the symptomatology necessitate different explanations.

Self-accusations, self-reproaches, self-devaluations, in the depressive, have to be understood by application of the structural viewpoint, with the superego as the frame of reference. One differentiation is obvious in the melancholic delusional ideas: the accusations are generally directed against the introjected object, although probably not all melancholic delusional ideas can be explained in this way. The superego phenomena appear in a different form in the symptomatology of depresion. To give a clinical example: In one of the sessions when my anorexia patient was describing her masturbatory fantasies with more than her usual emotional participation, she suddenly burst out with a childish exclamation: "You know that I was bad, I was very bad." Her "badness" was the masturbation, and what she expressed was the condemnation of the superego for her incestuous wishes. She produced much more frequently a different kind of self-devaluation in her repetitious complaints, expressing deep dissatisfaction with herself, especially with her body. The mechanism of this self-devaluation is quite different from the superego reaction to the masturbatory fantasies. Descriptively speaking the prevailing feeling there is that of a sinner, it is a feeling of guilt; in the complaints about the uglines of her body, there is deep sadness, or even despair. Is this type of depressive complaining or self-devaluation a superego reaction? I would think not. It is the expression of a perception based on the withdrawal of libidinal cathexis from the genital region and secondarily from the whole body. In other words, the content of the depressive complaints could be characterized as a generalized feeling of being castrated. I could repeatedly observe, during the analysis of this patient, a sequence which led to the narcissistic grief about her body. Describing it as it crystallized in the transference, the sequence was a reactivation of her incestuous libidinal wishes and their re-repression under the pressure of anxiety and guilt. When the new repression of her sexuality was completed, she was grieving about the deadness of her body. The driving force behind the repetitious complaints were certainly supplied by masochistic urges, but it was a desexualized masochism which appeared in her indulgence of self-pity and complaining. In this condition the complaints were at the same time appeals for love, appeals for soothing supplies from the outer world, appeals for the breast. The mnemistic imprint of the nursing experience, as recently described by Lewin (1950), might represent the nucleus of the idealized omnipotent parental images, that is, the consoling aspects of the superego.

The introduction of the structural viewpoint by Freud enables us to understand the impact of such competing parental images on the personality and on the symptomatology in the depression. In the clinical example which I have given, we see a cyclical process in which the forbidding superego curbs those libidinal drives that might bring the fulfillment of longings for loving and being loved, whereupon the depleted ego appeals vainly for consolation and bliss from the superego.

As a last point for discussion there is the problem of the chronology of the pathological structure formation. This problem often turns up in today's increasing interest in a correct evaluation and better understanding of the early developmental stages. The tools at our disposal for the solution of this problem are anamnestic data, which are not conclusive enough, and what is pertinent in observations during the analytical process. These observations allow us to form a precise picture of the dynamics of the neurotic process, but leave us in the darkness in regard to insight into the early phases. Where the preverbal stages are concerned, the possibility for recall is limited. For example, the material which I have on my anorexia patient would lead to the conclusion that life begins at five. That was the moment when her eating difficulties started, as I have mentioned, closely following the mother's pregnancy. The cannibalistic impulses which break through in her dreams refer clearly to this event. Yet one could recognize what might be called different geological layers in her oral impulses and fantasies. Oral-sadistic impulses coming through in dreams were directed against the body of the mother. They may have been of preoedipal origin; on the other hand, the drive pattern, to tear out "something" from the mother's body and eat it, in this patient at least, was clearly related to her penis envy. While oral-sadistic impulses directed against the mother's body are certainly present probably in the first year of life it seems that they become organized in a specific drive pattern in the girl much more definitely through experiences which increase penis envy.

Several analysts have remarked that the intensity of oral envy which appears with discovery of the anatomical sex difference creates in the girl particularly intense oral-sadistic reactions. The time element is important, and the nearer to the phallic phase such an event takes place, the greater is the possibility of a severe reaction.

There is probably in every individual a constitutionally determined variability for frustration tolerance. During the first year of life this frustration tolerance will determine the infant's reaction to hunger, pain, cold, etc. It will determine also the intensity of his longings for the nearness of the mother's consoling body. The frustration tolerance which certainly represents an innate predisposition is influenced by the experiences of the early life history and most crucially by the attitude of the mother to the infant. Depressive patients are undoubtedly people with a great need for the reassuring nearness of their love objects and a low tolerance for the frustration brought about by separation from the object. Very often in the anamnesis of depressives the evidence of early oral frustration is evident, but sometimes corroborative data of early frustration cannot be found. What every analysis of depressives shows clearly is the interrelationship between the dependency on the object and the ability to accept the sexual role in its given biological framework. In other words, there is a strong connection between separation anxiety and castration anxiety; this latter may possibly be corrected through a happy development, or the efforts of analytic therapy may overcome, or at least diminish, the impact of separation anxiety. In every endeavor to localize the chronology of a pathological structure formation we meet a remarkable feature of human development, namely, that development moves in two directions, back and forth; that earlier phases of development influence later phases, and that the later phases change the impact of earlier events. To exemplify the difficulties by a problem which is of general importance but especially pertinent for the the understanding of depression, I should like to bring up the question, in which way early oral conflicts may influence the severity of the superego. It is a possible assumption that intense oral-sadistic impulses contribute to a building up of a severe superego. But there are other possibilities too. Often, in analytic thinking we un-reflectingly assume that sadistic or aggressive ten-dencies are more pathogenic than purely libidinal drives. Yet this assumption is not necessarily valid. The intensity of oral-libidinal urges creates a greater need for the approval of the love object and thus leads to the necessity to curb impulses which jeopar-dize the good will of the love object.

As B. D. Lewin (1950) has shown us convincingly in his recent book, early oral experiences contribute to the development of masochistic needs, which in their turn may influence very definitely the severity of the superego. Masochism, an extremely complex drive pattern in men, must be understood as develop-ing out of variegated libidinal roots. Masochism has its independent origin, it is not merely sadism turned inward. Clinical observations show that in patients in whose instinctual life masochistic trends are con-spicuous the oral drive patterns are also unusually accentuated. Lewin put forward an idea which may explain this frequent coexistence of oral and maso-chistic trends. The experiences of nursing, the pleas-urable relaxation, the merging with the mother's body, may form one of the libidinal nuclei around which the complicated pattern of the masochistic instinctual drives are built. To the severity of the

[136]

superego, masochistic trends contribute decisively in their final form, that is to say, in the form in which they are molded through the vicissitudes of the oedipal situations. The impact of such masochistic drives on symptomatology and character will depend on the way in which the ego uses them. In depressive patients we see a severe superego blocking the way to the love object by curbing the genital sexuality, and then a shift from the grieving over this loss to the grief about the inadequacy of the self. The indulgence in self-pity and complaining is then a secondary masochistic gratification. If the mature form of the object relationship is blocked there may appear archaic oral longings for merging with the mother and the breast. Some aspects of the symptomatology in depression can be understood as the outcome of conflicts created around these archaic oral longings. Lewin's interpretation of insomnia could explain the frequent sleep disturbance in depression. Sleep, originally the sequel of nursing, assumes threatening significance. Such a change can go back to disturbances during infancy, but could be also the result of later complications. If the need for merging represented in sleep takes on strongly masochistic meaning, it has to be avoided. The root of the pathological disturbances may have to be sought in the earliest period of life, or it may emerge in later periods of development, but this does not present us with an "either-or" alternative. In principle, both possibilities must be assumed to be at work, and only the study of an individual case can give the answer which of these two possibilities is operating. Localization of the origin of anorexia presents us with the same theoretical difficulty: the nature of the oral drive pattern does not determine the symptom. Not all depressive patients with the same cannibalistic or oral-sadistic drives, with the same incorporative needs, develop eating disturbances. A complicated set of factors, not all of them necessarily recognizable, will decide whether or not an eating disturbance results.

In this paper the idea has been advanced that one finds that in producing the symptomatology of depression different mechanisms are at work. I believe that such an approach reflects the general state of psychoanalytic thinking in our days. We are much less apt to reach easy generalizations, but much more able to develop concepts and correlations which are descriptive of the unending varities of the phenomena presented to us by our patients.

BIBLIOGRAPHY

Abraham, Karl: (1924) A short study of the development of the libido. In: *Selected Papers on Psycho-Analysis.* London: Hogarth Press, 1942.

Eissler, K. R.: (1943) Some psychiatric aspects of anorexia nervosa. *The Psychoanalytic Review, 30.*

Freud, Sigmund: (1917) Mourning and melancholia. In: *Collected Papers, IV.* London: Hogarth Press, 1925.

Gero, George: (1936) The construction of depression. *International Journal of Psycho-Analysis, 17.*

Jacobson, Edith: (1946) The effect of disappointment in ego and super-ego formation in normal and depressive development. *The Psychoanalytic Review, 33.*

ANOREXIA

Lewin, Bertram D.: (1950) *The Psychoanalysis of Elation*. New York: W. W. Norton & Co., Inc.

Lorand, Sandor: (1943) Anorexia nervosa. *Psychosomatic Medicine, 5.*

Schur, Max and Medvei, K. M.: (1937) Über Hypophysenvorderlappen Insuffizienz. *Wiener Archiv für Interne Medizin, 31.*

Spitz, René A. and Wolf, Katherine M.: (1946) Anaclitic depression. In *The Psychoanalytic Study of the Child. II.* New York: International Universities Press.

Sylvester, Emmy: (1945) Analysis of a psychogenic anorexia in a four-year-old. In: *The Psychoanalytic Study of the Child, I.*

MANIA AND THE PLEASURE PRINCIPLE

Primary and Secondary Symptoms

M. KATAN, M.D.
Cleveland, Ohio

SINCE THE PUBLICATION of my article on mania comparing the meaning of the word in schizophrenia and in mania (1940),[1] my ideas on this subject have remained substantially the same. However, on two points my thinking has developed further: (1) I now find it necessary to divide the manic symptoms into primary and secondary ones; and (2) the role of the pleasure principle in the manic process has become clearer to me. At the end of this article I have appended a comparative study of the traumatic neuroses and manic-depressive disorders as they relate to the pleasure-pain principle.

[1] Because of the war situation, I had no opportunity to correct the proofs of this article, in which an unfortunate error occurred. Material which should have constituted the last three paragraphs of my discussion of mania appears on p. 142 in the midst of the discussion of the schizophrenic word. This error is a very disturbing one and of itself may cause the reader to desist, if not for other reasons.

I. *Primary Symptoms*

The primary symptoms are those which constitute the manic syndrome, namely, affect of pleasure, flight of ideas, and readiness to make decisions. In this article I shall try to show that in mania the pleasure principle is functioning under abnormal circumstances. Severe cases of mania are, of course, unsuitable for analysis, and therefore I have formed my opinion of mania by utilizing various impressions and observations.

Let me begin with a clinical impression which is shared by a number of other psychiatrists. This impression has resulted from a study of manic-depressive cases of the classic type, as well as various cases of schizophrenia which were colored by maniacal symptoms.

These cases have convinced me that manic symptoms are the result of an attempt at restitution. Even when improvement does not take place, the tendency toward recovery may still make its influence felt, for in such instances manic symptoms serve to slow down or to prevent a further development in a psychotic direction. As a general rule, acute schizophrenic states in which strong manic symptoms are present have a favorable prognosis. But in chronic cases as well, we have found that manic reactions may considerably retard the process of deterioration or even prevent it. Many cases of paranoia with a manic coloring show a strong tendency toward improvement. Even in those maniacal forms of dementia paralytica which are not treated, there is a good chance of spontaneous recovery of some duration. And in the manic-depressive psychoses, melancholia frequently passes through a manic stage before recovery takes place. Freud used this example in developing his ideas on mania. As we shall see, his concept implied that the transformation from depression to mania had already initiated the recovery. Thus the manic reaction would dispose only of the energy accumulated in the depression, which energy has now become superfluous.

This unmistakable tendency toward recovery in mania forms the basis of my metapsychological concept of mania. In defining mania as an attempt at restitution, I want to stress the fact that this attempt aims at restoring *normal* relationships. The maniacal attempt at restitution, then, is altogether different from the schizophrenic attempt at restitution. The latter attempt results in the formation of delusions, hallucinations, etc., which are an unrealistic way of resolving the conflict.

Next, I want to emphasize that in mania we find evidences of a return to the pleasure principle. The patient is engaged in a continual search for pleasure. His facial expression is such that he seems to be constantly prepared to break out into laughter. We know that the pleasure principle, during development, is modified into the reality principle. In mania, however, the reality principle is appreciably reduced, and thus we may say that the manic personality has regressed to a lower level of development. At the same time, it should be noted that this regression does not lead to an exact replica of the situation as it existed in childhood. Rather, we may say that in mania the pleasure principle is overdone. Manic patients derive pleasure from situations in which, objectively, there is no reason to find pleasure.

These facts, of course, have been known for a long time. In 1932 my wife presented a paper on optimism before the Viennese Analytical Society, in which paper she pointed out how strongly optimism relies upon denial as a defense (Angel, 1934). Bertram Lewin (1934) and Helene Deutsch (1933) have stressed denial in manic states; not only denial, but also projection and identification have been convincingly set forth by Helene Deutsch as being among the defense mechanisms in mania. In this connection we may say that projection and identification are equivalent to denial. A patient of Helene Deutsch's, in projecting aggression, denied her own aggression by accusing her analyst of being aggressive toward her. Another patient, in identifying herself with her analyst, denied her own weakness.

The manic patient, by experiencing certain situations as positive which are not positive at all, and by denying the negative character of other states, has removed himself to a greater or a lesser degree from the reality principle.

Another point about mania should be mentioned.

In the maniacal thought process, many associations occur according to the primary process. The secondary process has no longer a firm grip on the patient's trend of thought. Does this conclusion mean that in mania the primary process is functioning under its own power?

In my previous article on mania, I endeavored to show how every trend of thought which deviates from the secondary process is a compromise between the primary and secondary processes. One should not assume, however, that this compromise is the result of a contest between the relative strengths of the primary and secondary processes, for to make such an assumption is to overlook the forces which are trying to express themselves through these processes. For example, early in the development of psychoanalysis, Freud pointed out that in wit the ego deliberately makes use of the primary process in order to attain its goal; in other words, the primary process in wit is representative not only of the id but also especially of the ego.

The displacement in symbolism has a defensive as well as an id aspect. To the id, the symbol has the same meaning as the original. To the ego, the symbol means something different and therefore it can be used to ward off the original. Accordingly, in the aforementioned article I concluded that symbolism is used only if the ego does not permit the id to express itself freely. Symbols are never creations of the id alone.

In the dream, the primary process is used for another reason. During sleep, there is a tendency to withdraw the cathexes of all mental functions. However, if certain functions fail to give up their cathexes and thus are disturbing to the sleep, a tendency to protect the sleep sets in, which endeavors to get rid of the disturbing factors. It attempts to do so by affording satisfaction, through the dream, to the disturbing factors. The primary process is used in the formation of the dream.

The schizophrenic delusion is a result of the attempt at restitution. This attempt makes use of the primary process for its purpose.

Thus the differences between the various states in which the primary process prevails are created by the forces making use of that process. In our study of mania, therefore, it will be our task to discover the force which strives through the primary process to attain its goal.

Our first conclusion resulting from clinical observations is that mania represents an attempt at restitution. We are now ready to ask whether denial and the other defense mechanisms of projection and identification are reactions through which the attempt at restitution endeavors to attain its goal. Although in the attempt at restitution a defense mechanism may perform the important task of preventing a sliding back, still the defenses alone cannot be responsible for the tendency toward restoration.

Denial, projection, etc., are certainly not among

the basic processes of the pleasure principle, although they may play a protective role and help to defend the pleasure principle when its maintenance is threatened. Accordingly we may assume that the predominant pleasure principle itself carries with it the maniacal tendency to recovery. In order to prove this assumption, we must obtain insight into the functioning of the pleasure principle in mania.

Here we meet with a difficulty. In its normal development, the pleasure principle is modified into the reality principle. Therefore, it seems paradoxical that the original pleasure principle should return to power to help restore the reality principle. The way out of this paradox is suggested by the following reasoning. Keeping to our formulation that mania represents an attempt at restitution, we may conclude that the pleasure principle is confronted with the task of getting rid of something which prevents the proper functioning of the reality principle. As soon as this obstruction is removed, the reality principle can again hold sway.

In considering the reduction or even the disappearance of the reality principle in favor of the pleasure principle, we are justified in asking what happens to the superego. The superego, as the representative of reality, is the most important pillar of the reality principle, and the reduction of the reality principle may therefore be taken to mean that the superego is now seriously impaired.

Freud, in his first approach to the problem of

mania, tried to make use of a so-called normal example. If some poor creature's burden is taken away from him—for instance, through the acquisition of a large sum of money—he will manifest his relief: the pent-up energy, which is no longer necessary, will be discharged in pleasure reactions. When this example was applied to mania, it meant that the energy accumulated in depression was now freed and was discharged in the maniacal attack. Thus the initial step to recovery consisted of the change from depression to mania. It was the function of mania to get rid of the "remnants" (i.e., the pent-up energy) of the depression. In "Mourning and Melancholia" (1917) Freud's new thoughts about the superego were still in the process of development. It was his opinion that in depression the superego overwhelmed the ego, and that in mania the ego usurped the power of the superego.

We may ask whether this so-called normal example is in itself sufficiently clear to be applicable to such a complicated situation as mania. Moreover, the normal example presupposes that the conflict is resolved, and thus mania is regarded as a discharge phenomenon. But mania, as we have already seen, is not a state free from conflict, and therefore the normal example is not applicable at all. To repeat: at the basis of the normal example is a resolved conflict, whereas in mania the conflict is still unresolved.

Rado (1927) assumed that in mania the ego was related to the superego in the same way as the satisfied baby is related to the mother's breast. In my opinion, this idea is not acceptable at all. The picture of the contented baby bears no resemblance to the harassed manic ego, which seems to diverge in all directions. If the manic ego succeeds in finding peace at all, it is only for very short periods; the next moment the patient is already looking for new sources of possible satisfaction. I shall return to this important point later.

There is more to be said in refutation of Rado's idea. According to his speculation, the superego was a strong faculty which provided a satisfying protection for the baby-ego in mania. This picture is at variance with Freud's conception, in which the ego assumes command of the situation.

Because I find no evidence of a strong superego formation in mania, I cannot agree with those conceptions in which "humor"—as described by Freud (1928)—is cited as an example of the way mania functions: the man sentenced to death who, on his way to the gallows on a Monday, remarks, "Well, this is a good beginning to the week!" In this example the superego consoles the ego as an adult might comfort a little child, by pointing out how meaningless the world is. Yet the danger—the execution—cannot be avoided.

In the manic situation we find no trace of that admirable quality of "humor." No protecting superego consoles the manic ego with words of wisdom. Nor does the manic ego need them. Mania is an expression of the attempt at recovery, and from here we may go on to conclude that in mania this attempt is powerful enough to set up an interference in the conflict in order to resolve it—an interference which was missing in Freud's example of "humor."

We have now reached the point of examining the conflict in mania. To our disappointment, we have to admit that we know very little about it. We are better informed about the conflict in depression.

The following description of the conflict in depression may be given. The ego feels itself narcissistically wounded by some object in the outer world, the injury generally leading to an oral deprivation. The deprived ego then reacts against the object aggressively. For various reasons the aggression cannot be expressed, and the conflict with the offending object in the outer world is changed into an inner conflict: one between the superego and the ego.

One should not lose sight of the vast difference between the superego in depression and the normal superego. The fact that an outer conflict is changed into an inner one affords a clue to our understanding of the situation. What would the outer conflict have been like, had it existed? We know that depression is characterized by deep regressions. Therefore, very primitive reactions against the offending object would demand expression in this outer conflict, but the ego would not allow this. Such reactions would bear traits similar to those in prepsychotic development, for a severe depression is a state quite different in structure from that of the common neuroses; both clinically and theoretically, such depression is a final defense against the outbreak of melancholia, which name should be reserved for the psychotic form of depression. In a depression (nonpsychotic form) the ego wards off these "prepsychotic" attitudes toward the object, with the result that the superego treats the ego as if the ego were the offending object. Accordingly the tension between the superego and the ego in depression reflects these "prepsychotic" attitudes which were not allowed expression. Thus the superego is no longer an independent faculty which judges the inner situation objectively, but is forced to be the executor of the warded-off instincts.

Does the superego, in depression, reveal some of the reactions of very early normal superego development? Although in depression regressive material is used, I still think our answer must be a negative one. The normal superego does not have its origin in those conflicts which are the cause of the depressive situation, but, in its final state, results from a healthy striving to break the restraints of the oedipal phase in order to establish an independent relationship with reality of a much wider scope. It is quite possible that this process begins rather early so that the first stages of superego formation have a connection with preoedipal relationships.

We now find ourselves confronted with two specific problems:

I. What causes the change from the depressive to the manic state?
II. In the manic state itself, of what does the conflict consist and how is it made to disappear through the attempt at restitution?

Problem I

In depression, we may say that the ego, for various reasons, does not allow the discharge of aggression against an object in the outer world. It is possible that during the course of depression, either the aggression diminishes or the ego gains in strength. Freud assumed that after a certain time the aggression exhausted itself. However, with the disappearance of this surplus aggression, the conflict would no longer exist. In my opinion, the result would then be a cure without a transformation into mania, for in mania there is still a conflict. The manic symptoms, in fact, are the result of the attempt to resolve this conflict. The other possibility is that the ego becomes stronger and alters the situation, without at the same time being able to diminish the aggression. This increase in ego strength would make possible the transformation into mania.

These two possibilities are, of course, extremes. In practice, an increase in ego strength may occur simultaneously with a diminution of aggression, and such combinations may then lead to minor attacks of mania.

For the time being, we can say nothing more about the transformation of depression into mania than to make the ultimately vague statement that the ego is undoubtedly the cause of it.

Problem II

Let us turn our attention to the manic state itself, from which we hope to gain insight into the manic process as well as a clue to the reason for the change from depression to mania.

First, a remark about the contact of the manic patient with his environment. Although in severe cases this contact is very disturbed, nevertheless it is plain that the manic is turning again to objects in the outer world. This means that the manic, to a certain extent at least, has made an attempt to cope with an outer conflict instead of with an inner one, as in depression. Our next conclusion is that the attempt at restitution endeavors to resolve this outer conflict through use of the pleasure principle. The manic attempts to get as much pleasure as possible and to avoid discomfort.

The best way of investigating the manic process is to examine the patient's trend of thought. We have already observed that in maniacal thinking the secondary process has lost its position of command to a large extent and the primary process now appears in the foreground.

This is the point at which to see whether Freud's

ideas about "wit" can throw any light on the maniacal process of thinking. To summarize Freud's
(1905) conception of the formation of wit: a preconscious thought is for a moment submitted to the primary process, and the result becomes conscious. The
ego, by allowing the primary process to operate, is
spared any countercathexis, which would be necessary for the maintenance of the secondary process.
The amount of countercathexis which has been freed
is then used to produce pleasure.

The thought which has been previously warded off
can then be expressed in the form of wit. In this way
the conflict between the ego and the warded-off
thought is eradicated. For this reason I regard the
process of wit as leading to a discharge. We are struck
by the fact that the various faculties of the personality co-operate harmoniously in order to effect this
discharge. However, if under neurotic conditions
laughter is used as a defense and the warded-off tendency is not discharged, then, in my opinion, we
should *not* speak of a discharge, for the conflict is in
no way changed. The situation is no different from
one in which other affects are used by the ego as a
defense; for instance, the mechanism of the phobia.

For our purpose, we are particularly interested in
the process of aggressive wit. An aggressive thought,
which normally would result in a conflict with another person, has, through its expression in the form
of wit, become tolerable, and a conflict is avoided,

whereupon a discharge of the ego's countercathexis as well as of the aggression takes place.

The comparison which now follows between wit and mania is extremely important, because it permits us to gain new insight into mania. The formation of pleasure and the presence of the primary process are similar in both wit and mania. In mania, as well as in wit, the operation of the primary process leads to the release of countercathexis by the ego, which countercathexis is then used to create pleasure. But from here on, we find only points of difference between wit and mania.

Wit is a normal process. In wit, the pleasure principle assumes command again in order to effect a discharge, but the entire process is of only very brief duration. In addition, it should be emphasized that the ego conforms to the demands of reality and uses the pleasure principle to avoid conflict with reality!

In mania, the attempt at restitution is at the center of the process and aims at resolving the existing conflict with reality. To attain this goal, the mind falls back upon the pleasure principle. We may therefore expect the pleasure principle to obey other demands than those occurring in the case of wit. In mania, the conflict cannot be resolved in the same way as in wit.

In aggressive wit, we have shown that the conflict is resolved and that a discharge of both ego energy and warded-off aggression takes place. In mania, the situation is completely different: here the conflict is not resolved, and for this reason the assumption was made at the beginning of this paper that in mania the process of discharge, in the way that Freud conceived of it, does not occur. We are now ready to develop this point a little further. In depression, aggressive feelings cannot be acted out. We have already stressed the fact that if aggression after a certain time loses its strength, a return to normal relations (and not a transformation into mania) will logically follow. We may then conclude that in mania the ego must cope with the aggression remaining from the depression. How does the ego do this? In a subsequent example we shall see that a very strong aggression was present in the patient and yet that in his maniacal state the patient expressed relatively little of it. It may be said that in mania generally not nearly the amount of aggression is expressed which might be expected to be present.

At variance with this conclusion are those forms of mania which manifest themselves very aggressively; sometimes, in fact, they give way to explosions of aggression. Yet these cases do not seem to have a more favorable prognosis than nonaggressive manias. In fact, the reverse might even be true. We shall leave this important point and return to it later when we are better prepared to consider it.

To sum up: in mania, the ego does not seem to be satisfied, but dissatisfied, notwithstanding the inordinate amount of pleasure that it experiences. Never is the pleasure formation such that the ego is able to relax. At the same time, the warded-off tendencies are not discharged to the degree that might be expected. To put it another way: in mania, there is an abnormally large amount of pleasure formed and there is relatively little outlet for the warded-off tendencies. This discrepancy is in contrast to the process operating in wit.

We may ask whether the formation of pleasure is necessary to keep up the denial of the conflict created by the warded-off aggression. As we have already mentioned, denial is only a defense and does not eradicate the conflict. The explanation that the formation of pleasure occurs only to keep up denial contains no reference to the attempt at restitution, which I regard as mania's primary task. Already at this point we may assume that in mania the formation of pleasure performs the function of doing away with the conflict. If this is true, then we see the mind engaged in a concentration of effort to create pleasure in order to eradicate the conflict.

A woman patient with cyclic symptoms told me during an analytic hour that it did not matter what she said—that even if she spoke the truth, I still would not be able to use it. She said, "It doesn't matter what I say, but how I say it. It is as if the word, by being pronounced, changes. It comes from above [pointing to the top of her head], proceeds by various ways downward, arrives finally in my throat, and when it is pronounced, the meaning is gone. It has become shriveled; the sap is out of it; it is dried up." Since only a few moments before, this patient had spoken of a baby at the breast, it was evident that the word had the meaning of breast, which she wanted to give up only after she had emptied it.

This example shows how, in manic thinking, the word may have a significance in itself. The word is regarded as though it were the breast. The patient did not want to utter the word until after it had become meaningless to her; she did not want to give up the breast until after she had emptied it.

We may conclude that as long as the manic patient continues to cling to the use of words, the pleasure he derives from speaking has not yet reached a sufficient degree. As soon as the pleasure results in complete satisfaction, the point of satiation is reached and the patient can rest. In other words, mania has then come to an end.

To illustrate the degree to which aggression is mastered by manic symptoms, I shall cite the following unusual case. A patient, a mason by trade, was strongly attached to his mother, his father having died many years previous. The mother, however, preferred the patient's younger brother, who was more capable. At the age of nineteen, following his induction into the armed services during the First World War, the patient had his first maniacal attack, accompanied by a "Faxen syndrome." His cure appeared to be complete.

Ten years later, after the death of his mother, he married. A male relative of the bride's came from a distance to attend the wedding and remained for a few days at the home of the newly-weds. Almost immediately after his marriage, the patient became excited, beat his wife, and ordered his wife's relative to leave at once. This second attack followed the same pattern as the first.

After the patient returned home from the clinic, his wife became pregnant. The patient then found himself becoming increasingly depressed as the time for the baby's birth drew nearer. After the child was born, he could not bring himself to perform the father's function of registering the birth; others had to do this for him. One night he remarked to his wife, "I have made you deeply unhappy." Otherwise his behavior was not conspicuous, and he did not appear disturbed while at his work.

When the child (a boy) was six weeks old, the patient consulted his physician one Saturday morning because of mild eczema. It was too late for him to report to work afterwards, so he returned home and told his wife what the doctor had said. As his wife playfully lifted up the baby to let it hear the ticking of the clock, the patient suddenly grabbed the bread knife from the table and stabbed his wife a number of times in the breast; the wounds were so severe that it was necessary for her to be hospitalized for five weeks.

The patient was immediately taken to a psychiatric institution. On the third morning after admission, he exhibited the same symptoms as in the two previous attacks. Again he acted the fool, taking water into his mouth and threatening to spit at me, etc.

These three attacks have a common denominator. On the first occasion, the patient was forced to leave his brother alone with his mother upon induction into the armed services; the second time, his wife invited a male relative to stay with them during the first few days after their marriage; the third time, the patient's little son was the competitor. On the occasion of the first attack, the opportunity to carry out his aggression failed; at the beginning of the second attack, he beat his wife; the third attack brought on the impulsive act, for which he had obviously been prepared for a long time. We may assume that his remark to his wife that he had made her unhappy referred to a dream in which he had already performed the aggressive act against his wife.[2]

It is obvious that the aggressive impulse arose from a situation in which the oedipus complex played the main role. The fact that this oedipal relationship is the cause of the manic attack does not mean that the ensuing mania is based upon the oedipus complex.

[2] This assumption is borne out by the tragic story as reported recently in the Cleveland newspapers, of a mother who killed her young son accidentally. The mother, after being divorced, had remarried, and the court awarded the child to the father. On the day that she was to deliver the child to his father, she took the father's pistol, which was still in the house and which she was required to return to him, and played with the child. Not realizing that the pistol was loaded, she pulled the trigger, with disastrous results. To the police she stated that the previous night she had already dreamed the scene almost exactly as it took place the next day. It would lead too far afield to discuss here the relation between the dream and the act which followed.

I hope it will become apparent in the course of this article that mechanisms which are derived from the early child-mother relationship, and which have no connection with the oedipus complex, constitute mania.

This case demonstrates clearly that the patient's aggression was directed against the breast. The sight of his wife lifting up the child obviously aroused in him the expectation that his wife would give it the breast. This expectation in turn aroused his oral jealousy, which resulted in his overt aggression. We may assume that if this maniacal attack had taken place prior to the incident of the wife's holding up the child, the aggressive impulse would not have occurred, but at this particular moment the aggressive impulse took the weak ego by surprise.

We may conceive of this impulse in the following manner. Under normal conditions, there exist, in addition to those urges which are not permitted by the ego, many other urges which are not warded off. However, if contact with reality is so far reduced that only a few ties remain, the warded-off urges become of special importance, an importance which they do not otherwise have. The stronger the ego's wish to maintain contact with reality, the more important it is that the warded-off desires also try to establish contact with reality; from this standpoint, the warded-off desires may be said to work in harmony with the ego. If the warded-off desires are relinquished, then this tie with reality is broken too, resulting in a more or less complete loss of contact. One may say paradoxically that *these warded-off urges are not tolerated and yet are needed!* It is such situations that give rise to dangerous impulses. Let us take our present example. The ego was in a weakened condition because of the various emotional events to which it had been exposed. When the mother lifted up the child, a situation suddenly developed in which the patient's aggression against the breast was immeasurably increased and the ego let itself be overwhelmed by the instinct. Time was not available for the formation of mania, nor could the ego immediately sever its connection with reality and thereby dissolve itself. Vehement as this aggression was, it still contained a tie with reality.

We see from this case how effectively aggression remains hidden in mania. The case emphasizes, too, that in mania only a relatively small amount of aggression is expressed. Still, mania succeeds many times in bringing about a complete cure; i.e., the surplus aggression has disappeared.

A third example will introduce a new factor. This patient suffered from severe depressions. It is significant that during his early years he had been jealous of younger children whom he saw nursing. This patient was inhibited in his speech. Under the satisfying influence of alcohol, however, the inhibition disappeared and he was able to speak without difficulty. What was more, at such times he could not stop. He always compared his stream of words to the flow of urine. The change that occurred in this patient was caused by alcohol. The cause of the change from depression to mania is, of course, quite different, but the result is the same. In mania, the urethral factor comes as something wholly unexpected, for which our study of depression did not prepare us.

Let us try to formulate a theory using the conclusions which came to light from our study of the three examples. To begin with, we see that the manic patient tries to build up a continuous store of pleasure, but which supply—I want to stress this point again—is not sufficient to satisfy the patient to the extent that he can relax. Also, oral and urethral factors cooperate in producing this pleasure.

We may start with a striking hypothesis of Freud's concerning the origin of laughter. Freud points out that the distortion of the corners of the mouth in forming the grimace, which is significant of the smile, appears first in the satisfied and hypersatiated baby who gives up the breast as he falls asleep. "The grimace is thus a correct mode of expression, for it corresponds to the baby's decision to take no more nourishment and expresses, so to say, the feeling of 'enough,' or rather 'more than enough.' This original meaning of the pleasurable hypersatiation may have caused the smile—which, in any event, remains the basic phenomenon of laughter—to become related, during its further development, to the pleasurable processes of discharge."[3]

The manic patient, through speech, in which the word signifies the breast, tries to obtain satisfaction. Obviously, the pleasure derived from speaking has a strong relation to the period when the child first learns to talk. Many children experience an inordinate pleasure in learning to say new words, repeating them over and over until they have mastered them. This delight in talking should not be considered a wholly new development; it is in part a direct derivative of the pleasure that comes from sucking.

We may conclude that not only oral but also urethral factors play a part in the creation of pleasure. During the first months of life, there seems to be a close connection between oral and urethral processes. Frequently, after satiation, the baby urinates. We know, too, that in adult life, laughter (which, according to Freud, is the derivative of the smile after oral satisfaction) can be accompanied by the urge to urinate and can even lead to incontinence.

We must distinguish sharply between the urethral factor in the sequence of breast feeding and urination during the beginning of life, and later sources of urethral stimulation. For instance, in the symptom of bed wetting, urination can be a strong expres-

[3] Freud, Sigmund: "Der Witz," *Gesammelte Schriften*, Vol. IX, p. 164. I have tried in this quotation to correct the faulty translation as it appears in *The Basic Writings of Sigmund Freud*, p. 733. Modern Library.

sion of masculinity as well as of femininity. These meanings are first apparent when problems of bisexuality begin to play a role. Yet I want to stress the connection between the intake of the contents of breast or bottle and the discharge of urine as it occurs in the beginning of extrauterine life.

Turning our attention again to manic patients, it has seemed to me significant that they are more interested in their urine than in their feces. For instance, one manic woman urinated in her teacup; another manic patient played continually with the water faucet; etc. In this connection mention should be made of the experiments conducted by Wiersma (1933), which showed that manic patients secrete urine much faster than melancholic patients.

Clinical observations of patients have yielded no consistent results. The evidence of increased urethral erotism is clear in one case but not in another. Still it seems that manic speech in general has a urethral meaning. It is therefore my conclusion that the process is displaced from the urethral zone to the mental processes, and in this way speech acquires a urethral meaning.

I do not think that one should consider the rapid secretion of urine a result of the tendency of all physiological and mental processes to be speeded up; rather, the reverse takes place. Analytical investigation points indisputably to the fact that the manic trend of thought has the same meaning for the patient as the flow of urine. Thus I consider the heightened urethral activity one of the basic phenomena of mania. One might remark here that in many neurotics this urethral factor is active also, especially in those cases dominated by the tendency "to get it over with," which the patients apply to all situations and which tendency they think is caused by their anxiety. In all such neuroses the urethral erotism is warded off by the ego, and the pleasure connected with the process is not permitted. Obviously, the ego is too weak and must take the warded-off urethral factor into its organization, whereupon the defense of "getting it over with" is established. In mania we find a completely different situation. The formation of pleasure is the goal because this pleasure is needed. For this reason the urethral process is used to an excessive degree by the pleasure principle—not, of course, in its original form (the secreting of urine) but in displacement to the mental processes, where it finds a wide field of application. The urethral pleasure is displaced to the mouth, adding superlatively to the pleasure derived from other oral activities. In this way the ego creates a situation where the pleasure derived from these functions becomes fully conscious. The use of the primary process in the manic trend of thought makes it possible for this trend of thought to symbolize the oral (sucking and drinking) and the urethral functions.

Although displacement to the mental functions does take place, it should not surprise us to find remnants of the original reaction in the accelerated discharge of fluid in mania.

We may go a step further and say that the words can represent objects. We have already seen that the word can have the meaning of breast. A patient with hypomaniacal symptoms continued to wet the bed over a long period in his childhood. Although his mother did not scold him when he did this, he was aware of the disgust in her face. And yet he continued to wet the bed. The pleasure that came from wetting was intensified by the warmth of the urine. As a child, he dreamed repeatedly of lying on the warm body of his mother, and then he would awaken wet. The warm urine and the warm body had therefore the same meaning. From this example and other ones we see that urine may connote an object.[4]

These considerations lead to the idea that in mania an object may be orally incorporated into the body and leave through the urethra. The introjected object is a fluid one, and according to Wiersma's experiments (1933), in mania fluid is much more quickly expelled than in depression. We may therefore say that the circulation of the object through the body occurs in a quick tempo. This assumption

[4] Here is another example to show that urine can represent an object. The father of a patient was, for professional reasons, absent from the home for many years during the patient's early childhood. During this period, when the patient was six years old, his mother died. His longing for his mother continued. He was able to satisfy this longing by permitting urine to enter his penis, yet he did not want to lose a drop of the urine. Although this patient did not show any manic reaction, his urine nevertheless became for him an object, and discharge meant the loss of the object.

is still in agreement with the conclusion mentioned at the beginning of this paper that the manic patient tries to give the introjected object back to the outer world, and in doing so he tries to transform an inner conflict into an outer one. We should add that the object is given back to the outer world for only a very brief time and then is introjected again, for the manic ego is not yet able to deal with the outer conflict adequately. This whole process is repeated over and over.

At this point I should like to remind you of Abraham's statement that the pleasurable intake of new impressions corresponds to a quick and pleasurable expulsion of what has been scarcely taken in, and that these processes of introjection and expulsion may be observed also in the flight of ideas. Abraham (1924) pictures the objects passing in rapid tempo through the patient's "psychosexual metabolism" (p. 472).

Yet the most important task in mania, as I see it, is the production of pleasure. The deprivation from which the ego suffers in depression, and which deprivation perhaps always goes back to an oral one, can become neutralized through this pleasure. When the point is reached at which the deprivation is completely neutralized, the aggression (which was caused by the deprivation) and the resulting introjection of the object are no longer necessary and the patient may be considered cured.

Sometime ago Dr. Edward Bibring presented what

seems to me a very clarifying idea, namely, that depressed feelings result from the ego's state of powerlessness. I think that in mania the ego regains its lost power to the degree that the original wound is healed through the constant production of pleasure.

I should now like to return to the problem of what causes the change from the depressive to the manic state (See p. 151). With the appearance of the urethral factor in the foreground in mania, we may conclude that *when depression changes into mania, the introjected object changes from solid to fluid.* Despite what appears to be clinical evidence to the contrary—I shall discuss this particular type of aggression shortly—I want to stress that *the orality in the manic attempt at restitution is characterized, not by biting, but by drinking or even sucking.*

This idea is supported by observations on alcoholism. When the alcoholic is engaged in a drinking bout, food frequently becomes unimportant to him. The same patient may have periods when he does not drink at all but instead indulges in "overeating." A patient of mine once volunteered, "If one is not permitted the satisfaction of sucking at the breast, then he wants to destroy the whole organ." Yet it seems to me that still another reaction is possible, namely, that the patient tries to get possession of the breast by incorporating this organ. I am inclined to think that it is especially the latter mechanism which is represented by overeating in alcoholism.[5]

[5] See also (d) *Aggression,* pp. 177-182.

We may now venture the following hypothesis. In the depression, behind the façade of tension between the ego and the superego, an interesting process is taking place. The ego attempts to regain its strength.[6]

6 In what follows I shall try to explain how the ego might regain its strength. Because the depressed patient places so much emphasis upon the inner conflict between the superego and the ego which is identified with the object, the conflict with objects in the outer world tends to disappear. Considered from this angle, the depression has a denial-like function. See Robert Waelder's ideas on denial (1951).

We may say that in the depression there is a trend "away from reality which is too painful." Thus the narcissistic wound inflicted by the object is less exposed to outside stimuli, and the ego, which is no longer continually irritated by the narcissistic wound, may to a certain extent recover.

It is true that the ego submits to tortures by the superego. But these the ego has deliberately brought upon itself. Through its identification with the offending object, the ego turns away from objects in the outer world and tries to shut out surprises by them, which surprises might otherwise arouse the id and thus lead to dangerous impulses.

This process of excluding painful influences from the outer world is much stronger in the psychotic form of depression (melancholia) than in the nonpsychotic form. Next to the psychotic layer in melancholia is always a nonpsychotic one. In the psychotic layer, contact with reality is relinquished and the outer conflict is eradicated. In the patient's nonpsychotic layer, contact is maintained with the outer world and we find here a nonpsychotic depression. Therefore, in melancholia two forms of depression are always overlapping: one, nonpsychotic; the other, psychotic. Those conflicts that cannot be mastered by the nonpsychotic form of depression must be taken care of by the psychotic form. The content of both types of depression is the same, although they differ in form. We find a similar situation in states of delusional jealousy, where always a neurotic form of jealousy is present as well.

I arrived at these ideas through studying Schreber's delusion about the end of the world. This delusion, of course, is a wholly different type of example from the ones we have been considering. Schreber was continually exposed to the danger that the men in his environment would arouse his excitement, which in turn would lead to masturbation. He therefore developed the delusion that the men whom he saw, and who tended to arouse him sexually, were not really there. At the end of two years he was able to suppress his erections completely. The danger that the men in his environment would eventually cause him to masturbate therefore disappeared. From then on, he no longer

[169]

If the balance of power swings in favor of the ego, the depression is cured. I want to repeat that I do not think the diminishing of aggression is particularly responsible for the increase in ego strength, which is then purely relative, but rather that the ego itself is improved. In this connection I wish to quote Dr. René A. Spitz (1951, p. 267) in his report on the recent panel on mania. Dr. Spitz "is inclined to confirm this assumption on the basis of his observations on the recovery from anaclitic depression. There the return of the love object actually represents a reinforcement of the ego, accompanied by a sudden temporary upward swing of the previously separated infants' developmental quotients, as published in my article 'Anaclitic Depression,' The Psychoanalytic Study of the Child, II, 1946, p. 340."

If, however, the warded-off instinct gains in power, the psychotic depression—namely, melancholia—may result.

There is still a third possibility. The ego may be able to bring about a regression of the oral activity from biting to drinking or sucking, and in this way the original pleasure principle is restored.

The formation of pleasure is what effects the

---

needed the delusion about the end of the world and he made what to him was a surprising discovery—that the world still existed! In this way the delusion about the end of the world served as a protection to Schreber's ego, which was now free to concentrate on suppressing erections. We see that in the depression the conflict between the superego and the ego enables the ego to gather strength for its encounter with the outside world, just as Schreber's delusion enabled his ego to win the fight against his erections. See Katan (1949).

cure. This pleasure comes from what I call a "total" reaction: ego and id are not working in opposition to each other, but, as we have already discussed, the ego needs and makes use of the id. The result of this manic attempt at restitution is the development of primary symptoms: manic affect, flight of ideas, and hyperactivity (in which the same principle operates as in the flight of ideas).

This "total" reaction needs closer examination in regard to the problem of discharge and the relationship between the latter process and the conflict. In the "total" reaction, ego and id work in close cooperation and both ego- and id-energies are discharged. But our next conclusion contains a surprise, for which we are not prepared: contrary to our expectation, this process of discharge does not lead directly to a solution of the conflict with which the manic patient is struggling. It is the aggression in the id which must be diminshed in order for the conflict to be eradicated, and we now see that the discharge of energies does not include, or at least not substantially, the id-aggression![7] The aim of the attempt at restitution, in effecting a discharge of id strivings, is to enable the ego to derive pleasure from it. This pleasure, in healing the narcissistic wound, causes the surplus id-aggression to disappear, and when this point is reached, the conflict is resolved.

It may further our insight to compare the process

[7] For an explanation of this statement about aggression, see pp. 177-182.

of discharge in mania with that, for instance, in the schizophrenic hallucination. At once we see a striking difference. In the latter the energy of the unconscious feminine urge, which causes the conflict, is withdrawn and then used to form a hallucination. The energy is therefore discharged, and for a certain period the conflict has been made to disappear (Katan, 1950, 1952).

Turning now to the role of the ego in the manic attempt at restitution, the purpose of this attempt is to enable the ego to derive pleasure. This restitutional process therefore operates as if it were wholly a function of the ego, through which function the ego tries to regain full command of the situation. One might at first glance consider this process comparable to the production of an affect as a defense, as, for instance, in the example already mentioned of the role of anxiety in the phobia. Yet the difference between the two processes comes immediately to the fore. Whereas the anxiety in the phobia has only a defensive task, the formation of pleasure by the ego in mania goes far beyond that, in striving for a cure.

In the form of the "impulse" which we have already discussed, we find also this same close co-operation between ego and id; here, however, the co-operation works to the advantage of the id only. Although the goal—maintaining contact with reality —is reached, the price paid is too high.

We know that in a number of other processes, such as "wit" and "symbolism," the ego and the id cooperate closely also. Yet these processes occur under normal conditions; whereas in mania and in the "impulse" previously described, the co-operation between ego and id takes place on a deeply regressive level.[8]

II. *Secondary Symptoms*

Such "total" reactions, which aim at recovery, need to be protected against disturbing factors. Obviously the ego is the origin of these special mechanisms. Among them are denial, identification, projection, aggression, exhibitionism, and buying sprees. Manic symptoms may therefore be divided into *primary ones,* which are the result of the attempt at restitution, and *secondary ones,* which aim at protecting this basic attempt. The secondary symptoms are not the result of defense mechanisms in the true sense of the word. Generally ego defense mechanisms ward off the demands of the id or dangers from the outside. In the secondary symptoms, the mechanisms employed by the ego endeavor to protect the restitutional process, in which there is close co-operation between the ego and the id. In this special case I therefore prefer to use the term protective mechanisms instead of defense mechanisms, for among the desires that find expression and need to be protected are those originating in the id.

The ego therefore participates in two functions

[8] The problem involved in these processes deserves, of course, much more intensive discussion. I hope to do this at some future time.

which are closely related to each other: the primary attempt at restitution, and the secondary protective mechanisms. Let us briefly review these protective mechanisms.

(a) *Denial*. In mania the ego tries again to establish contact with reality. The conflict which causes the depression is not solved by the mere transformation of the depression into mania. An attempt is made, however, to change the inner conflict into an outer conflict again. Many manias, of course, are not preceded by a depression; the situation is obviously such that from the very beginning an outer conflict is maintained.[9] The attempt at restitution aims to create pleasure in order to neutralize the narcissistic wound. It derives this pleasure from the oral incorporation of the object and from the urethral expulsion immediately following. This process is symbolically represented by the flight of ideas. In the latter, the object, which is represented by the word, is the same as in depression, with the exception that the object is submitted to a mechanism different from that in depression.

If this manic attempt at restitution were forced immediately to cope with the outer conflict in its full

9 If mania were really a reaction of triumph over liberation from the burden of the depression, it would be difficult to explain its occurrence in those cases where no depression had been present. The ego would then be triumphant because it had prevented the occurrence of a depression, and mania would constitute a discharge of energy before the energy could be pent up in a depression. The expression of triumph over liberation from a burden which has not yet been felt does not seem very likely.

[174]

strength, the chances are that the whole attempt would break down at the very beginning. Therefore, protection by the ego sets in: the ego denies the existence of the conflict or at least tries to devaluate it. Whereas denial is clearly an ego reaction, in the flight of ideas mechanisms are at work which are derived from the phase of very early development when it is difficult to differentiate, in the introjections and expulsions, between ego- and id-reactions. Thus we observe two layers: in the more superficial one, denial of the conflict takes place; in the attempt at restitution, not only is the conflict fully recognized but also an attempt is made to solve it.

It is appropriate to ask whether, in the analytic therapy of hypomania, it is desirable to try to destroy the mechanism of denial through interpretations to the patient, for with the disappearance of denial, the process of recovery loses one of its strongest protections. Fortunately in analysis, much more occurs than the mere interpretation of denial, for the ego is confronted with all possible aspects of the conflict. By working through the various aspects, the ego not merely is persuaded to relinquish denial but is enabled to solve the conflict in a more realistic way. In the hypomanic case described by Helene Deutsch (1951, p. 271), we see clearly that when denial no longer was possible because of changes in the environment and at the same time the inner situation remained unchanged or even became worse, the patient found her escape in suicide.

[175]

(b) *Identification.* As an illustration, we may take another of Helene Deutsch's examples. The patient's father originally had been a wonderful, very much admired man but later became an alcoholic, a "dirty bum." In the patient's depression, his identification with the worthless father stood out in the foreground, whereas in his maniacal state the patient identified himself with the father whom he had greatly admired. Helene Deutsch has therefore extended Freud's famous statement characterizing the depression—"the shadow of the object has fallen on the ego"—by remarking that in mania "the light of the object has fallen on the ego."

Adapting this example to our own purposes, we may begin by repeating that in mania the conflict is not yet resolved. When the patient recathects a wonderful childhood relationship with his father, we may conclude that he does so in order to deny the existing conflict with the "bad" father. For this reason—and this is the only point on which I differ with Helene Deutsch's article—I cannot see how the narcissistic tide which rose during the manic phase was supported by the superego. In my opinion, the identification with the ego ideal, in addition to increasing the ego's narcissism, also served the function of a denial. Such a process does not point to a superego function but to what I should call a protection by the ego of the attempt at restitution. For this reason I think that the identification with the much admired father, although the latter is an ideal for the ego, still takes place in the ego and not in the super-ego.

This ego identification with the greatly admired father has no connection with the "fleeting" identifications as they occur in the flight of ideas. In the latter we see the exponent of the attempt at restitution, which, in order to attain its goal, introjects and expels the "bad" object. However, in the protective mechanism the ego identifies itself with the "good" object. Through the increase in narcissism as a result of this identification, the ego is better able to protect the attempt at restitution against disturbing influences.

(c) *Projection.* There is nothing to add to what has already been said, namely, that projection is used in a way equivalent to denial.

(d) *Aggression.* We have finally reached the point where we shall want to draw a conclusion about the role of aggression in mania. According to our theory, the manic attempt at restitution attempts to heal the narcissistic wound which originally caused the depression. In mania, the cure is not effected through a discharge or acting out of aggression, despite clinical evidence of aggressive behavior in mania. Fortunately, certain manic cases even support our theory that mania causes aggression to disappear. I have already cited the example of the man who had a lot of aggression but who was harmless in the manic attacks.

Here is another example of the same type. A

woman in her sixties lost her husband, who had dominated her during her married life. She was quite
composed until the day after the funeral. Then the
picture of her deceased husband aroused her aggression, and she allowed his pet bird to escape. That
night she waited for her death. The next morning
she destroyed her false teeth and then tried to throw
them down the drain. Immediately following this incident, she developed a state of manic delirium in
which aggression was completely lacking. After a
number of months, when she was sufficiently improved to have a new false plate made, she again became tense when the teeth were ready, and they
therefore were not given to her. Nevertheless, mania
returned in full force. We are justified in asking
whether this patient originally destroyed her "biting
tools" in order to ward off oral aggression. Afterwards her mania took over.

Let us now turn to those cases of mania where the
aggressive attitude prevails and consider the example
which Dr. Jacobson (1951) cited in the discussion, by
way of refuting my theory. "Dr. Jacobson brought
the patient out of her depression by a number of
hypnotical suggestions, upon which the patient reacted with a mania. During the first session the patient made sucking movements. Later she was
aggressive. The patient then told Dr. Jacobson
amiably, with a sadistic expression, but without ag-
gressivity, that though she was devouring everything,
nothing happened to anybody or anything" (p. 275).

Dr. Jacobson meant that a denial mechanism had been developed which made both the outer world and the patient herself invulnerable.

In the discussion, I pointed out that the first response of the patient had been sucking and not biting. We may now look for a further explanation. Obviously, the patient's desire for satisfaction from sucking was not fulfilled, whereupon she expressed her aggression by biting. But her aggression was intended to do no harm. I think this feature of "harmless aggression" not only is an expression of the "protective" mechanism of denial but also, and primarily, represents an attempt to get hold of the object, which she needed in order to realize satisfaction from her desire to suck.

Here is another example. A manic woman patient, with hysterical tendencies, was referred to a well-known woman analyst, who could not accept her for analysis but advised her to consult a man analyst. In a discussion with the doctor who had originally referred her to the first analyst, the patient reported her misfortune at not being accepted for treatment, remarking sneeringly, "If she had only known that I wanted, before leaving, to bite off her breasts . . . !" Previously the patient had undergone a long period of treatment with a woman psychiatrist, who, after repeated begging by the patient to be allowed to suck the psychiatrist's breasts, gave in to the patient's wish; the patient then discontinued treatment. It is irrelevant whether the psychiatrist actually gave in to the patient's wish or not; the story at least clearly reveals the patient's own wish. Again in this example I do not regard the desire to bite off the breast as a blindly destructive one but as a wish to possess the breast. In this wish the patient is trying to possess the organ in order to obtain satisfaction from it—not in order to destroy it.

After I had discussed with Dr. Douglas Bond some of my ideas on mania, he observed two manic cases which both began with the patient's drinking excessively large quantities of water, as well as alcohol. From this observation we might proceed to a consideration of the dry condition of the mouth existing at the onset of mania; however, I am not ready to discuss this problem yet.

We may improve our understanding of the manic process considerably by recognizing that the lack of satisfaction from the primary desire to suck (eventually to drink) creates a danger: this lack of satisfaction may lead to an increase in the feeling of oral deprivation, which may then result in a return of the depression. In order to ward off this danger, the ego tries to keep the door open, at least, to the possibility of obtaining satisfaction in the future from the desire to suck at the breast. The aggression expressed in mania, therefore, is an ego reaction to get hold of the breast in order to protect the maniacal attempt at restitution. This reaction prevents the conflict, which has still to be resolved, from again increasing. The aggression in mania is newly formed by the ego and acted out at once. This ego reaction, therefore, does not lead to a diminishing of the amount of aggression warded off in the unconscious. To state the same conclusion a little differently: the aggression released in mania is not a discharge of aggression residing in the unconscious; the situation in the id is not changed at all.

Therefore, the ego uses its aggression to secure possession of the desired object. Its primary aim is not to harm the object but to exercise power over it. As a generalization, one may say that ego aggression can be aroused by anything which tries to interfere with the attempt at restitution. Yet the warded-off aggression in the unconscious is wholly destructive. The maniacal attempt at restitution even sets in to master this unconscious form of destructive aggression by healing the narcissistic wound, which otherwise would continue to stimulate the destructive drive.

However, when the ego is still too weak to make these strenuous efforts to protect the restitutional process, the ultimate aim of obtaining satisfaction through sucking cannot be maintained. The aggression of the ego then acquires more and more the characteristics of revenge in wishing to destroy the object; i.e., the aim of the aggression becomes the same as that of the warded-off aggression. The situation is then ripe for either an impulsive discharge of destructive aggression or the return of the depression because the aggression must be warded off.

Clearly, in severe cases of mania, efforts by the ego in the attempt at recovery, as well as in the protection of this attempt, can lead to exhaustion. I do not agree, however, with Dr. Jacobson's opinion that this exhaustion is caused by the discharge of agression. Again I repeat my theory that mania is not a process of discharge of destructive aggression, but an attempt to control this destructive drive. When the attempt is successful, the conflict tends to diminish, thus making ego energy available for the more normal functioning of the ego. Compared with the normal ego, the ego in mania is weak and *extremely narcissistic;* compared with the ego in depression, it has already gained in strength.

(e) *Exhibitionistic Tendencies.* Manic patients try to draw attention to themselves in all possible ways. It is a common sight in a hospital ward to see them adorned with ribbons, etc. Manic patients, especially women, who expose themselves naked are by no means rare. Whatever the motivation for their exhibitionistic behavior, I think these manic patients all have one aim in common: to show off, from narcissistic needs. One should not confuse their attitude with a craving for love. Manic patients have not progressed this far; even if they receive love, this love does not neutralize the conflict. The increase in their narcissism serves mainly to protect the attempt at restitution. At the same time the fleeting relationship which is created by the patients' exhibitionistic behavior adds also to the denial of the conflict with the object.

(f) *Buying Sprees.* Manic patients are conspicuous for their inability to resist the temptation to buy things which they do not need at all. They are always ready to spend more money than they have. They want to satisfy their "narcissistic hunger." Sometimes they become actual kleptomaniacs.

In addition to buying things for themselves, manic patients will often shower gifts on others. This activity affords them a narcissistic satisfaction. The same symptom is manifested by children who steal money in order to buy presents for their friends; in contradistinction to manic patients, these children are motivated by the need to be loved. If manic patients seem to demonstrate this same motive, then it is, of course, only a superficial reason for their behavior, the deeper reason being a narcissistic one.

"Object hunger" is often mentioned in connection with mania. This phenomenon, which is clearly demonstrated in the patients' exhibitionistic behavior, as well as in their other attempts to attract people to them, is nothing more than a desire to satisfy their narcissism.

Considering the protective mechanisms as a whole, we may ask again whether the protective character is not a sign of a superego function. Upon looking closely at the various mechanisms, we conclude that "denial" and "narcissism" are the two which come to the fore and which certainly cannot be conceived of as functions of the superego. Even the identification with an admired father figure seems to me to be in the service of the mechanism of denial. It is therefore my opinion that the deeper layers of the ego in mania, which are in close co-operation with the id, are involved in the attempt at restitution, whereas other parts of the ego carry on the function of protecting the attempt at restitution.

Denial serves mainly to devaluate the existing conflict; the increase in narcissism is a protective measure against the damaging influence of this conflict.

Suicide

Taking a look at the manic reaction as a whole, we may conclude that mania offers much better protection against suicide than the depression does. Yet sometimes suicide occurs even in mania. In this connection I want to make one more comment about depression: severely depressed patients are generally hospitalized and for this reason are already protected. They also have strong defenses against the danger of suicide, but these we shall not discuss here. It is a known fact that the depressed patient who is improving is much more exposed to this danger. The depressed patient who leaves the doctor's office feeling much better and then commits suicide a short time afterwards is not an uncommon case clinically. When the patient first ventures to re-establish contact with outside objects, he is in a vulnerable position. His sensitivity makes him feel easily rejected, and this state constitutes a dangerous factor which may cause him to commit suicide. Suicide in mania may have a similar origin. When rejection takes the manic patient by surprise and his protective mechanisms are off guard, he may suddenly find himself exposed to suicide.

Classification of Mania

Can we still agree with the traditional psychiatric opinion that mania is a psychosis? To answer this question, we must determine, first of all, just what is meant by a psychosis. Of prime importance is the fact that in a psychosis a break with reality has occurred. Generally a psychosis is preceded by various symptoms, which differ markedly from the common neurotic symptoms but have one trait in common with them: they still maintain contact with reality. This period I call the prepsychotic phase. If definitely psychotic symptoms, such as delusions, are present, it should not be assumed that the symptoms characteristic of the prepsychotic phase have disappeared. In such circumstances I regard these latter symptoms, which can no longer be called prepsychotic in the true sense of the word, as belonging to the nonpsychotic layer of the personality. I have chosen this name nonpsychotic because these symptoms cannot be called neurotic nor do they come under our definition of a psychosis.

Returning now to our question, we may say that severe cases of mania are so at odds with their environment, are so far removed from objective reality testing, that they have to be hospitalized. On the basis of these considerations, which are primarily of a social nature, we may call mania a psychosis. By doing so, we are making a "social" diagnosis, which is not the same as a diagnosis based upon "scientific" insight. The latter emphasizes the fact that mania is an attempt to regain normality, i.e., to re-establish contact with reality. According to "scientific" insight, then, manic symptoms do not fit within the frame of a psychosis but have a strictly prepsychotic or nonpsychotic character.

After reaching this conclusion, we shall want to consider the typical characteristics of the prepsychotic phase. Drawing from my studies of schizophrenia, I wish to stress that the most prominent symptom in the schizophrenic prepsychotic phase is the loss of the positive oedipus complex. After this loss (in the man), the urge toward femininity comes into the foreground. With the dropping out of the oedipus complex, changes in the homosexual urge become apparent. In the perversion, or as a warded-off trend in the neurosis, homosexuality is centered around the positive oedipus complex. In both of these latter states, homosexuality is a defense against the demands of the positive oedipus complex. By contrast, homosexuality in the prepsychotic phase, through the loss of this complex, has a much less complicated structure. The ego wards off the homo-sexual urge with such defenses as are still available. When these defenses can no longer be maintained, contact with reality is broken off.

One must keep in mind that although homo-sexuality in the prepsychotic phase is warded off, on the other hand it constitutes the last tie with the object. This object is even the representation of the ego or the ego ideal. Therefore, any factor which can cause the dissolution of this last tie will be con-sidered disastrous by the ego.

We are now ready to consider to what extent traits are noticeable in mania which are comparable with traits in the schizophrenic prepsychotic phase just described. Is the oedipus complex lost in mania, too? In my previous article on mania (1940), I defended the point of view that although mania may some-times be caused by a conflict originating in the oedi-pal sphere, mania itself is not rooted in the oedipus complex. Heterosexuality in mania can many times be demonstrated to be of a very weak and superficial nature. In the dreams of the manic patient, the heterosexual expressions are scarcely able to cover up the homosexual desires.

The maniacal mechanisms which we have dis-cussed are certainly not of an oedipal nature. The mechanisms essential for mania have their origin in the oral phase (sucking), at a period when one cannot yet speak of the existence of an oedipus complex. The child-mother relationship forms the basis of mania. True, these mechanisms may sometimes be expressed in relationships that appear to derive from the oedipus complex. Yet the analysis of manic patients reveals that man and woman become identical: the man's mouth is analogous to the vagina, the penis to the breast. Identifications with both parents are then basically alike.

As far as loss of contact with reality is concerned, we have already discussed the fact that mania is an attempt to prevent or to repair such a break with reality. We may therefore conclude that mania is a true prepsychotic development. It is even possible that mania has the same basic conflict as the schizophrenic prepsychotic state, although such an assumption has yet to be proved by further investigation. Nevertheless, the manic reaction is completely different from the prepsychotic ego mechanism of defense in schizophrenia. On the other hand, the existence of the same basic conflict in both states would explain the fact that manic as well as depressive reactions are not limited to a sharply defined and separate group (the manic-depressive psychoses) but also occur, in various forms, in the broad group of schizophrenias.

Mania and Depression

Let us take a last look at the relation between mania and depression. Mania does not ward off depression. Neither are mania and depression merely two different ways of dealing with the same conflict.

There is a much more intricate relation between these two types of reactions.

It is the task of depression to stem the tide created by the outer conflict by transforming this into an inner one. In this way, as we have already discussed, a protection is formed against harmful influences from the outside. Thus the ego gets a chance to regain its strength. This strength is necessary to establish a manic reaction. Depression and mania therefore comprise two successive steps in the same process: in depression, a tendency prevailing to "hold the line" while preparing for a change into mania; in mania, a tendency to "regain lost territory." Of course, as we have already discussed, a patient may recover from a depression without passing through the manic stage, or mania may develop without a preceding depression.

Still another point deserves consideration. When a depression does not afford a sufficient defense, melancholia may arise. In the latter illness a break with reality occurs comparable with that in schizophrenia. In melancholia the attempt at restitution leads to a solution of the conflict by unrealistic means, namely, delusions.

We reach the conclusion that in contrast to depression and melancholia, mania does *not* show a differentiation into a prepsychotic and a psychotic form. Delusions are not a manic symptom. Whenever they do occur in the course of mania, they are a sign that the manic syndrome has developed within the frame of another mental illness, e.g., schizophrenia, paranoia, an organic psychosis, etc.

What causes this difference between mania, on the one hand, and the combination of depression-melancholia, on the other? In my opinion, this difference results from the fact that mania attempts to restore normal relations through the use of the pleasure principle. Therefore mania cannot lead to solutions excluding contact with the outer world, for such solutions would result in delusion formation.

Instead of developing further details about mania, I have chosen to append a comparative study, which affords a broader treatment than the subject calls for.[10]

---

[10] In order to keep within the limits of an article, I have not discussed the various interesting viewpoints developed by Bertram Lewin (1950), whose viewpoints differ considerably from my own ideas about mania. Neither have I mentioned some ideas developed in my previous article (1940), which ideas I still hold valid. In that article I worked out my ideas on introjection much more extensively than in the present article on mania.

The Traumatic Neurosis, Manic-Depressive Disorders, and the Pleasure-Pain Principle

In the following study I want to work out certain ideas concerning the relation between mania and depression, on the one hand, and the pleasure-pain principle on the other. Freud (1924) referred to the latter principle as "the watchman of our mental life" (p. 255). Our question is: what is wrong with the functioning of this principle in manic-depressive states?

Let us examine comparative material. It may be helpful, first, to consider what happens when a trauma directs a damaging blow at the pleasure principle. By studying the vicissitudes of this principle after the occurrence of the trauma, we may be able to gain insight into the problem which now confronts us.[11]

The trauma takes the patient by surprise; consequently he is not prepared for the danger, and his defenses break down. The proper functioning of

11 In the discussion of the traumatic neurosis, I shall follow, except for the explanation of the conversion symptoms, the ideas developed by Freud in *Beyond the Pleasure Principle.*

the pleasure principle is seriously impaired, and this impairment gives rise to the patient's symptoms. In his dreams, under great anxiety, the patient again experiences the trauma. The impairment of the pleasure-pain principle makes it possible for the more primitive repetition-compulsion to exert its influence by causing the trauma to appear in the dream. The ego, which in its surprised state did not have time to develop anxiety, tries to make up for this lack of preparedness by developing a strong anxiety in the dream. In this way it fulfills its wish to be in a state of preparedness again; in other words, to place the pleasure-pain principle again in command. But even in the dream the pleasure-pain principle is not in complete command, for then it would exclude the influence of the repetition-compulsion.

The very limited extent to which the pleasure-pain principle is actually in command is demonstrated by the patient's reactions to contact with reality. The defenses are shattered, and the ego is unable to concentrate on any particular task. Contact with reality causes the patient intense pain. When the ego tries to utilize its functions, the cathexis of these functions impresses us as greatly reduced and soon exhausted. These less-cathected functions are secondarily libidinized, and the resulting symptoms are similar to hysterical conversion symptoms. The patient develops disturbances of the senses; for example, concentric limitation in the visual field; absence of feelings of pain upon the usual neurological examination; sometimes an inability to "think decently," i.e., sexual thoughts popping up instead. In addition, there may be nausea, even vomiting, dizzy attacks, lack of co-ordination in walking, etc.; in short, a variety of symptoms, all fitting within the frame of a severe conversion hysteria.

Yet the differences between hysteria and the traumatic neurosis are the inordinate amount of suffering and the shattering of defenses in the latter illness. Furthermore, in hysteria the ego functions are sexualized by the warded-off urges; as a result of this sexualization, the ego secondarily relinquishes its functions so that the id is now in full possession of them.[12] In contradistinction to this hysterical process, in the traumatic neurosis the ego is affected first; then, after the shattering of the ego defenses, the urges from the id are enabled secondarily to libidinize the ego functions.

Thus, in the symptoms, the aroused sexual urges are bound. As soon as these symptoms are formed, they become secondarily of great value to the ego: they prevent a return to the situation where danger threatened. The crucial point is that these symptoms were not originally developed for the purpose of withdrawing from the danger, but once formed, they are used for this purpose.

12 See Freud's article "Psychogenic Visual Disturbance according to Psychoanalytical Conceptions" (1910), and Chapter I of *The Problem of Anxiety* (1926).

We know that when the trauma has inflicted serious bodily damage, a traumatic neurosis is very unlikely to occur. The ego cathects the injured spot, and this concentration of narcissistic energy counteracts the shattering effect which the trauma might otherwise have on the ego defenses.

We may conclude that the ego uses the injury of the body secondarily in the same way as it uses conversion symptoms in the traumatic neurosis, namely, as a protection against a re-exposure to the danger that threatens life.

This brief review makes clear two things. First, just as the victim of a traumatic neurosis develops anxiety in his dreams in an attempt to restore the pleasure-pain principle, so in mania the patient strives to produce pleasure in order to restore this principle to normal functioning. Second, the depression and the traumatic neurosis appear to have a common element in the painful suffering experienced by the patient. Freud (1920) observed that the traumatic neurosis, in its strongly marked signs of subjective suffering, resembles hypochondria or melancholia (p. 8).

Let us discuss the depression first. The patient has been subjected to a psychic trauma. He is consciously—if at all—poorly informed about the trauma and gives the impression of having had no or very little "pain" reaction at the time the trauma occurred. There would be no reason to suspect that he had been exposed to a traumatic event if it were not for other symptoms which he develops. He acts, not as if he were wounded by an object in the outer world, but as if he were suffering from an "inner" wound.

The complaints resulting from this "inner" wound take up his entire thinking. It is common for many depressed patients to repeat their self-accusations over and over again, under great suffering. It is relatively easy in most cases to discover from the self-accusations that the original traumatic blow does not come from the inner world but has been inflicted by an outside object. It is clear, therefore, that the depressed patient is unable to keep the traumatic event completely out of his consciousness. He succeeds merely in disguising the trauma which is the cause of his illness. We may conclude, then, that the constant repetitions are the result of the repetition-compulsion; the ego is not strong enough to shut out the influence of the latter and reacts to it with great suffering.

At first glance, it seemed as if the point of comparison between the traumatic neurosis and the depression was the similarity in suffering in both illnesses. In the traumatic neurosis the ego defenses are shattered. That is the reason why contact with reality is so painful; it is like rubbing salt on an open wound. The similarity in suffering leads us to ask whether in the depression, as well, the trauma has shattered the defenses.

In order to answer this question, it is necessary to

reconstruct the whole course of events. We already know that the ego is poorly informed about the trauma and does not react to it with pain. This fact leads us to conclude that from the very beginning the trauma has been worked through primarily in the unconscious. If the ego had had the defense of "pain" at its disposal, it might have been able, through withdrawal, to avoid being wounded. What actually happens, however, is that the wound inflicted by the object alters every faculty of the personality, mainly through deep regressions. In the resulting situation the ego is confronted with the problem of how to handle the aroused aggression. To do this in a mature way is already from the very beginning out of the question. Furthermore, for various reasons, the ego is unable to discharge its aggression against the object. The ego, lacking the strength to handle the conflict with the outside world, changes the outer conflict into an inner one. Thus a flight to the inner world takes place, and from this withdrawal result, secondarily, the typical symptoms of the depression. This ego reaction of withdrawal marks a fundamentl difference between the depression and the traumatic neurosis.

In the traumatic neurosis the symptoms are the result of the shattering of the ego; they are used secondarily, as we have seen, for the purpose of withdrawing from the danger.

In contradistinction to this process in the traumatic neurosis, the ego in the depression, although unable to cope with the object in the outer world, now puts up an active defense by transforming the outer conflict into an inner one. It is an attempt on the part of the ego to protect itself against the dangerous contact with the outer world. This proves that the pleasure principle is still in command, for this avoidance reaction belongs to the pleasure-pain principle (an avoidance of painful stimuli). Therefore, in the depression, the ego's defenses are not shattered, and the painful suffering in this illness must have another source than that of the pain reaction in the traumatic neurosis. Thus, as far as the origin of the suffering goes, our initial assumption that the traumatic neurosis and the depression both have suffering as a point in common is not correct.

We have now clarified our insight into the situation. The ego in the depression does not have pain at its disposal and is therefore unable to prevent the influence exerted by the offending object from becoming traumatic. Secondarily, after the trauma has already proved effective, the ego engages in an avoidance reaction by changing the outer conflict into an inner one. However, through this change the ego does not get entirely rid of the trauma, for the latter, under the influence of the repetition compulsion, reappears, although with this one difference: it is now repeated as if it originated from the inner world. To this inner trauma the ego reacts with pain, which pain reaction was lacking when the trauma originally occurred. We may therefore conclude that the ego tries to change its state of unpreparedness to one of preparedness. Viewed from this angle, *the production of painful affects by the ego in depression is as much a part of the attempt at restitution as is the production of pleasure in mania.*

Our conclusion is that the attempt at restitution utilizes the repetition compulsion. The latter keeps the ego in constant contact with the inner trauma. Through this contact the ego is continually stimulated to produce "pain." We may assume the ego is afraid that similar traumatic events will occur again. In anticipation of such events, aggression is aroused against the outside object, which aggression is immediately turned secondarily against the ego and thus represents an increase in the danger of suicide. The ego reacts to this aggression with adequate suffering. This increase in suffering, we discover, forms a defense to keep the ego from being surprised by an offending object. If, notwithstanding this defense, suicide still occurs, we may conclude that the suffering was not strong enough to ward off this disaster.

When the (nonpsychotic) depression is unable to erect the necessary defenses, (psychotic) melancholia sets in, in which state the conflict with the outer world can be much better eliminated than in the depression. But this is not the place to probe more deeply into this problem.

At what point does the transition from depression to mania occur? We may conclude that when the point is reached, in the depression, that the ego suffers more pain from its inner conflict than it would suffer from the outer one, it is ready to turn again toward the outer world. The ego has now recovered to the extent that it is prepared, if necessary, to react again with a sufficient amount of pain to the outer conflict. At this point the ego is ready for the transformation into mania.

In mania we find the second step of the attempt at restitution. The manic patient is not satisfied but is attempting to become satisfied. To attain this end, the ego employs mechanisms to produce pleasure in order to compensate for the lack of it. We have already mentioned the similarity in conditions under which anxiety is formed in the dream in the traumatic neurosis, and pleasure in mania. In mania also, the repetition compulsion brings the conflict to the fore and stimulates the ego to react to it. One may observe in mania, even more clearly than in the depression, the use made of the repetition compulsion by the attempt at restitution. The manic patient attempts to get rid of the conflict and, in this attempt, endeavors to eradicate the influence of the trauma which caused the manic-depressive disorder. Yet there is this difference: the patient with a traumatic neurosis must surrender to the influence of the trauma, whereas the manic patient has a good chance of overcoming it. The former patient can restore the pleasure principle only in dreams, when sleep excludes the still too painful influence of reality. The latter patient does not need sleep to aid him in his attempt at recovery, but acts while fully awake. This fact at least proves that in mania the pleasure principle is strong enough to heal the narcissistic injury.

We have now reached the point where we are able to consider the results of our comparative study of the traumatic neurosis and manic-depressive disorders. In contradistinction to the traumatic neurosis, the ego's defenses in manic-depressive states are never shattered. This means that the pleasure-pain principle has still the upper hand. Yet its weakened condition is clearly demonstrated. In neither depression nor mania are the defenses able to cope with the conflict on the basis of the *reality* principle.[13] This principle—which is only a modification of the pleasure principle—is abandoned and the more primitive pleasure-pain principle is restored. It should be emphasized that this restoration of the pleasure-pain principle is not merely a regression, for much more than regression takes place.

In this respect we are able to see a similarity as well as a difference between manic-depressive disorders and the traumatic neurosis. In the latter the pleasure-pain principle is interrupted because the trauma has struck at the defenses at a moment when they are unprepared. In the manic-depressive disorders the pleasure-pain principle is not interrupted, but damaged, for the defenses, although not altogether unprepared, are prepared insufficiently. During the initial contact with traumatic events, *not*

[13] This statement is worked out on pp. 204 ff.

enough pain is produced to cause an immediate avoidance reaction before the stimuli can become traumatic, but neither is there a sufficient production of pleasure to counteract successfully the influence of the traumatic events. This means that the ego is unable to cope with the trauma either by running away from it or by neutralizing its effect. Both depression and mania are evidence of the attempt at restitution. By the overproduction first of painful affects in depression, and then of pleasure in mania, this attempt endeavors, in two successive steps, to restore both fundamental features of the pleasure-pain principle to a state of sufficient preparedness.

It is clear that the attempt at restitution uses the pleasure-pain principle in an effort to heal its own wounds, so that this principle is in a state of continual hyperfunction. What do we know about this self-curing process? In order to gain information, let us look again at the maniacal process, for not only is this the primary subject of our study but it appears to offer better possibilities than the depression.

In mania the attempt at restitution effects a cure through the pleasure-pain principle. For the time being the reality principle cannot be maintained. The influence of reality has modified the pleasure-pain principle into the reality principle. On the one hand, reality counteracts the need for immediate satisfaction; the realization of satisfaction is postponed, although it still remains the goal in the remote future. On the other hand, an avoidance reaction cannot follow immediately upon the first contact with painful stimuli. Reality forces the personality to submit to many painful stimuli before satisfaction can be realized.

Here a question arises. Obviously, if through regression the original pleasure-pain principle is restored, the reality feature—namely, the postponement of both immediate satisfaction and immediate avoidance—is abandoned again. Accordingly one might expect to find in mania, where the pleasure principle is doing "extra work," not only a heightened search for satisfaction but also an increased avoidance of painful stimuli. This is even more true because the manic patient has turned again to the outer world in an effort to solve the existing outer conflict.

Yet we have observed that the search for pleasure is not accompanied by too great avoidance of the painful outer world. The solution of this behavior may be found in our prior discussion of the secondary symptoms. It is their task to protect the attempt at restitution. By denial or devaluation of the conflict, the ego tries to create a situation in which the manic attempt at restitution does not have to cope immediately with the outer conflict in its full strength. In this way the ego, by creating secondary symptoms, becomes less sensitive to painful stimuli from the outer world, i.e., it reduces the avoidance reaction. The attempt at restitution therefore works in a conspicuous way: it stimulates one aspect of the pleasure-pain principle and tries at the same time to reduce the other in order to prevent the avoidance reaction from setting in too soon.

One may ask now whether this process, as we have outlined it for mania, is applicable also to depression. Here we are confronted with a difficulty: the regression from the reality principle to the pleasure-pain principle does not seem to be present in depression as it is in mania. In depression there is a clearly marked superego, and this latter faculty may be conceived of as one of the pillars of the reality principle.

We have already noted the great difference between the superego in depression and the normal superego. The power which any superego, normal or abnormal, has at its disposal arises, of course, from the id instincts. But the normal supergo acquires its aims through identifications, especially those with the parental figures. From our previous discussion we know that the superego in depression loses these mature aims and that through this loss the normal objective and "steering" qualities of the superego, which contribute materially to the proper relationship with reality, are abandoned. The instinctual reactions against the offending object—reactions which have a deeply regressive character and which are warded off by the ego—now express themselves secondarily through the superego. These superego aims therefore acquire the features of the warded-off id instincts and secondarily give rise in the ego to very painful affects.

[203]

After the ego's failure to prevent the offending object from inflicting damage to the pleasure-pain principle, the attempt at restitution takes over. We must realize that in order to change the situation from a state of insufficient preparednes to one of adequate preparedness again, the formation of painful stimuli by the superego is required, whereupon the ego reacts with painful affects. We have already discussed the fact that the ego is now less exposed to the harmul stimuli from the outer world and in this way gets a chance to increase its strength again. At the moment when the ego is strong enough, the transition from depression to mania takes place, and the ego is no longer passive but assumes an active attitude toward the outer world.

Returning now to our question: Is the reality principle maintained in depression, or has the pleasure-pain principle taken over? The superego remains only as a form. Its content (i.e., its aims) is detached from reality and comes under the command of the id. This form (of the superego) has lost its independent character and is now purely a means in the restitutional process, which has as its goal the production of painful affects by the ego. This restitutional process is carried on by the pleasure-pain principle. Therefore we may conclude that the pleasure-pain principle has taken over. What remains of the reality principle is drawn, through a regressive process, into the pleasure-pain principle and becomes a part of it.

Our next question is: What organic process gives rise to the pain? We have seen that in mania the oral (sucking) and urethral functions are the source of the pleasure formation. In depression it is possible that the function of the entire intestinal tract is the source of the pain formation.

Let us take as an example a case of conversion hysteria. The patient had attacks in which his jaws and the muscles around the esophagus were contracted, following which he had diarrhea. Analysis revealed very plainly that these symptoms were based upon the idea of eating his wife in order to punish her. This interpretation, in fact, was given by his own wife, long before I analyzed him, when she remarked to him, upon observing his symptoms, "Now you are eating me again!" This patient did not have a genuine depression because the object which he was busy destroying remained a foreign body. The process did not lead in the least to an identification and therefore is much simpler. That is the reason why I have used it as an example.[14] In depression, on the other hand, the suffering of the ego is brought about by identification with the object which originally should be tortured.

In manic-depressive disorders it is better to think in terms of regression not merely to certain erogenous zones but to entire tracts. Thus in mania the oral-renal-urethral tract is involved; in depression,

[14] This example demonstrates clearly that oral incorporation and identification on an oral level are two different processes.

the entire intestinal tract. In the maniacal attempt
at restitution we have observed close co-operation
between ego and id. Partial instincts of the id are
used so that the ego may derive pleasure from them,
which pleasure is necessary for the restitutional process. We discover that the attempt at restitution in
depression follows the same pattern, although at
first sight it may seem to be more complicated. In
depression also, instincts of the id, in particular
aggression, are used so that the ego may derive painful affects from them, but they are conducted along a
detour. Via the superego, they are directed against
the ego, which then reacts with the pain necessary to
avoid further conflict with the outer world.

In both depression and mania the pleasure-pain
principle is utilized by the attempt at restitution. In
fact, the attempt at restitution is identical with the
effort of the pleasure-pain principle to regain full
command. In mania the avoidance reaction, upon
meeting painful stimuli, is counteracted primarily
by denying the pain. One may ask whether in depression, where the pain is so prominently in the
foreground, there is not a force working simultaneously against the search for pleasure. I think
we may assume the presence of this counteracting
force from the fact that the libidinal attachment
to the offending object—which attachment would
otherwise seek satisfaction—has now been used in
forming an identification with the object. As soon
as the ego regains sufficient strength again, it resumes

the search for pleasure. In depression, as well as in mania, one part of the pleasure-pain principle is hyperactive, and the other part reduced, although in the two states the parts are of course interchanged.

Through our metapsychological exploration we have gained enough insight to advance the idea that the manic-depressive disorders occupy a place quite distinct from all other mental illnesses—the neuroses as well as the psychoses.

We shall have to limit ourselves to generalizations. The neuroses reveal clearly the strong influence of reality in their inception. Neurotic symptoms are the result of various conflicting forces. These symptoms may be regarded as the expression of a state of equilibrium, and when one of the forces changes, then a new balance has to be found. Yet no attempt at restitution seems to be at work in the neuroses, and many times the avoidance of pain is more in the foreground than the search for pleasure.

Next let us consider schizophrenia, for this is the most important of the psychoses. It is necessary to distinguish between the prepsychotic phase and the psychosis proper. In the prepsychotic phase, the overwhelmingly strong urge toward femininity in the male patient is a threat to his masculinity. Accordingly an avoidance reaction sets in, which leads to the severing of contact with reality. In the subsequent psychosis this contact remains severed, and the attempt at restitution now strives for a solution of the conflict by unrealistic means. Delusions, etc., are the result. We may regard this psychotic process, which I have described here without going into any details, as following the general pattern of the pleasure-pain principle. Of necessity, avoidance of the dangerous stimuli has the upper hand and causes the attempt at restitution to take an abnormal course. The affective disorders are different from all other mental illnesses. They embrace a wide field, ranging from moods deviating only slightly from the normal through all possible gradations to the most severe attacks of mania and depression. They are evidence of the weakness as well as the strength of the pleasure-pain principle. Weakness is shown by the fact that the manic-depressive disorders cannot be prevented. Strength is demonstrated by the attempt at restitution, of which the symptoms are the result. The pleasure-pain principle repairs its own damage through depression and mania. However painful these processes may be for the patient or however abnormal they may appear to observers, they are still proof of the ceaseless effort of the pleasure-pain principle to carry out its task as guardian of life.

BIBLIOGRAPHY

Abraham, Karl: (1924) A short study of the development of the libido. In *Selected Papers on Psycho-Analysis.* London: Hogarth Press, 1927.

Angel, Anny: (1934) Einige Bemerkungen über den Optimismus. *Internationale Zeitschrift für Psychoanalyse, 20.*

Deutsch, Helene: (1933) Zur Psychologie der manisch-depressiven Zustände. *Internationale Zeitschrift für Psychoanalyse, 19.*

—— (1951) Panel on Mania and Hypomania. Abstracted in *Bulletin of the American Psychoanalytic Association, 7.*

Freud, Sigmund: (1905) *Wit and Its Relation to the Unconscious.* New York: Moffat, Yard, 1917.

—— (1910) Psychogenic visual disturbances according to psychoanalytical conceptions. In *Collected Papers, II.* London: Hogarth Press, 1924.

—— (1920) *Beyond the Pleasure Principle.* London: Hogarth Press, 1922.

—— (1924) The economic problem in masochism. In *Collected Papers, II.* London: Hogarth Press, 1924.

—— (1926) *The Problem of Anxiety.* New York: W. W. Norton & Co., 1936.

—— (1928) Humour. In *Collected Papers, V.* London: Hogarth Press, 1950.

Jacobson, Edith: (1951) Panel on Mania and Hypomania. Abstracted in *Bulletin of the American Psychoanalytic Association, 7.*

Katan, M.: (1940) Die Rolle des Wortes in der Schizophrenie und Manie. *Internationale Zeitschrift für Psychoanalyse, 25.*

—— (1949) Schreber's delusion of the end of the world. *Psychoanalytic Quarterly, 28.*

—— (1950) Schreber's hallucinations about the "little men." *International Journal of Psycho-Analysis, 31.*

—— (1952) Further remarks about Schreber's hallucinations. *International Journal of Psycho-Analysis, 33.*

Lewin, Bertram D.: (1934) Analyse und Struktur einer passagèren Hypomanie. *Internationale Zeitschrift für Psychoanalyse, 20.*

—— (1950) *The Psychoanalysis of Elation.* New York: W. W. Norton & Co.

Rado, Sandor: (1927) Das Problem der Melancholie. *Internationale Zeitschrift für Psychoanalyse, 13.*

Spitz, René A.: (1951) Report on the Panel on Mania and Hypomania. In *Bulletin of the American Psychoanalytic Association, 7.*

Waelder, Robert: (1951) The structure of paranoid ideas. *International Journal of Psycho-Analysis, 32.*

Wiersma, E.: (1933) Die Psychologie der manisch-depressiven Psychose. *Psychiatrische en Neurologische Bladen.*

INDEX

[211]